PRE-PUBLICATION REVIEW OF
HEALING THE MIND THAT CAN'T LET GO

By Russell Meares, Emeritus Professor Psychiatry, at the University of Sydney.

This is a wonderful book! It tells the remarkable story of Michael Masani's successful treatment of a man who had suffered a disabling depression for more than twenty years, despite multiple forms of therapy. The therapy was of an original kind consisting a combination of "trance, story, and voice," coordinated in the context of an empathic, non-intrusive, and flexible relationship. The outcome was a restoration of the feeling of "flow" and the capacity for enjoyment.

The therapeutic focus was on feeling states, "the very stuff of life." It is our internal feeling milieu, Masani states, "that shapes and colours our thought patterns and behaviour — not vice versa." Unique features of the book are the quality of its language and the skill in its construction. The author weaves into the story his patient's treatment, that of the referring psychiatrist, and parts of his own personal background. The theory of treatment is supported by references to the scientific literature in a way which does not dull the liveliness of the narrative. The language is clear and lucid. Complex concepts are effortlessly distilled into brief, apparently simple, formulations.

Michael Masani's use of words and the voice is sophisticated, highly developed. He states: "My only instrument is my voice... its effect is through resonance and pattern recognition rather than through reason. Storytelling, with its limitless capacity for imagery, analogy and metaphor, is a great facilitator." He sees therapy as facilitation. "Carefully crafted stories" using allegory and symbolism "reverberate throughout our nervous system" triggering "a cascade of self-healing, and self-generating responses."

This book might signal a breakthrough in the therapy of treatment resistant depression, a major psychiatric problem. Masani's account will be of great value even inspiration, to those trying to help people suffering the endless pain of this disorder.

Russell Meares, Emeritus Professor Psychiatry, at the University of Sydney. Recent books include, *The Poet's Voice in the Making of Mind*, *Intimacy and Alienation: Memory, Trauma and Personal Being* and *The Metaphor of Play*.

HEALING THE MIND
THAT CAN'T LET GO

Ground-breaking discoveries that

transform our understanding of depression,

its causes and the path back to life:

this book changes everything.

MICHAEL MASANI AND 'DARREN'

First published in 2021
Copyright © Michael Masani 2021

The moral rights of the author have been asserted.

All rights reserved. Except as permitted under the Australian Copyright Act 1968 (for example, a fair dealing for the purposes of study, research, criticism or review), no part of this book may be reproduced, stored in a retrieval system, communicated or transmitted in any form or by any means without prior written permission. All inquiries should be made to the publisher.

Publisher: Syandra
Chapman, ACT 2611
Australia
Phone: (61 2) 6287 1710
Web: www.syandra.com.au
Email: michael@syandra.com.au

Primary print ISBN: 978 0 6452594 0 7
Ebook ISBN: 978 0 6452594 2 1

A catalogue record for this book is available from the National Library of Australia

Cover design by Ralph Cavero
Typeset by Working Type
Printed by Ingram Spark

The material in this publication is of the nature of general comment only, and does not represent professional advice. It is not intended to provide specific guidance for particular circumstances and it should not be relied on as the basis for any decision to take action or not take action on any matter which it covers. Readers should obtain professional advice where appropriate, before making any such decision. To the maximum extent permitted by law, the author and publisher disclaim all responsibility and liability to any person, arising directly or indirectly from any person taking or not taking action based on the information in this publication.

*This book is dedicated to my wife, Deb.
I am eternally grateful for your loving kindness,
unwavering belief, relentless editing
— and for the long rich conversations.*

Acknowledgements

I am deeply grateful to the following people who have all contributed to making this book possible:

Kate Kituai whose patience and skilful tuition persuaded me I could write when all the evidence said otherwise. 'Kate's Kitchen' is in every page!

My brother, Peter, whose great interest in the mind lit a flame in my young heart.

St John Miall and Alexia Miall for your friendship and constant support.

My meditation teachers, Walter Bellin, Gita Bellin, Robert Meredith, Roger Harman and the late Robert Prinable. They were heady days.

Frank Wright and Greg Brice who introduced me to P.S.H. therapy.

Professor Russell Meares whose being, writings and lectures have sustained me over many years.

Contents

Foreword		1
Chapter 1:	*Michael and Darren*	7
Chapter 2:	*Depression — No Ordinary Sadness*	17
Chapter 3:	*A Complicating Factor*	33
Chapter 4:	*Don't Mention the Feelings*	47
Chapter 5:	*The Brain That Can't Let Go*	63
Chapter 6:	*The Tigers Keep Coming Back*	81
Chapter 7:	*My Own Person*	101
Chapter 8:	*The Four Faces of Anxiety*	117
Chapter 9:	*No Moorings*	131
Chapter 10:	*Voices in the Head*	149
Chapter 11:	*Feathered Away*	165
Chapter 12:	*Don't Ask Me to Change*	181
Chapter 13:	*The Halfway House*	197
Chapter 14:	*The Emerging Self*	213
Epilogue		233
Endnotes		249

Foreword

This book delivers a much awaited breakthrough in our understanding and treatment of depression. Some may find it controversial.

As a practicing psychiatrist for many years, I know too well the debilitating effects that depression and anxiety have upon people, destroying lives and relationships. Alarmingly, the incidence of these conditions is increasing. Pharmaceutical interventions and talk therapies are not always effective cures.

For nearly 20 years I was the consulting psychiatrist to the person known in this story as Darren. An intelligent man in his late forties, depression had brought about a collapse of his marriage and ended a promising career. These events only served to worsen his condition. Rarely did I witness him reveal the depths of his despair, preferring, as he would, to put on a best face. He found it hard to accept that he was sick and thought of himself as a fraud. His dark humour was a way of expressing his self-contempt.

Many attempts were made to improve his condition. Darren was not responsive to anti-depressant medication and he gained little benefit from weekly sessions of talk therapy. In no way was this a reflection on the quality of help he was receiving. His psychologist, Anne, is highly regarded within the profession and has had many years' experience working with deeply traumatised patients. She and I would discuss Darren's condition and after one particularly difficult episode I recommended a course of Electroconvulsive Therapy (ECT). But seven sessions of ECT made little impact on his condition.

I recall instances involving Darren that illustrate the confusing and often destructive nature of his depression. The first occasion was a time when my wife was preparing to enter a local fun run. I accompanied her to a preparatory training session that Darren was conducting for members of the public. This was Darren's great love — training people to run. For an hour or two I remember watching him energised, animated and interacting with members in the group. He was a different person, one who had temporarily escaped from his illness. Inevitably he collapsed an hour or so later, victim once more to his own demons.

Around this same time, Darren was participating in a CIT course, hoping to qualify as a sports coach. By all reports he was doing well and the possibility of his gaining a new career in an area he seemed to love filled us all with hope. Suddenly and without reason, Darren withdrew from the course. I never knew why.

Anne suggested referring Darren to see Michael Masani, whom she knew was getting good results with a therapy called Private Subconscious-mind Healing (P.S.H.). She described what she knew of this therapy as part hypnosis and part mindfulness, with elements of storytelling — a method sufficiently different to anything we had tried previously. Darren was wary and took his time to decide to go through with it. It was his nature not to undertake anything unless he was sure he could commit to seeing it through.

Eventually Darren did commit and began weekly sessions with Michael. I continued to see Darren on a monthly basis. Over time I noticed his mood getting lighter and there was less talk of his self-loathing. I knew things were definitely improving when, without prompting from me, Darren asked if I could renew his referral to see Michael for a further three months.

As Darren's condition improved, he talked about 'growing emotional ears.' Darren was unexpectedly able to understand much that had previously confused him. He was remembering things Anne and I had said in the past that now seemed to bring him comfort. This therapy appears to have an ability to allow people to hear, accept and understand concepts which they could not hear, accept or understand when in the depths of depression.

Darren's tendency to over analyse every thought and situation meant that the cognitive reasoning of talk therapies was not the best process for him. The P.S.H. approach allowed light to shine where previously it had been restricted by feelings of not deserving, not being good enough. Any form of therapy that provides an alternative route for people to see and feel their innate goodness is to be celebrated.

I am particularly drawn to the references in the book about our innate self-healing properties. Much of this healing occurs naturally while we sleep (in particular during REM sleep) when the brain is able to process difficult and powerful emotions triggered by recent experiences. Should this autonomic process fail for any reason, our emotions are left raw and become the seed of future anxiety. Michael explains how P.S.H. therapy mimics this process of night time therapy, essentially catching the painful feelings that had previously fallen through the cracks. It is through a combination of what he calls voice-guided meditation and a certain type of storytelling that sets the brain's innate healing and regenerating processes in motion.

Darren's story gives us a rare glimpse into the secrets of the human mind. As Darren himself might say, how the garden of the self can recover and even flourish after being smothered in weeds for a lifetime. Whether you are a mental health practitioner or someone affected by mental illness, I urge you to read this book. You will gain a more compassionate understanding of depression, and you will find profound implications for the future direction of therapy. I have devoted my life to helping people recover from mental illness; I believe this book can inspire a new generation of more effective and empathic treatments for people with depression and anxiety.

Don Lawrence, M.B.B.S. (Syd), D.P.M. (Lond), F.R.A.N.Z.C.P. (Ret'd) Ballina, NSW.

Dr Lawrence passed away in 2020 a few months after writing this forward. He is survived by his wife Jenny, who has generously given us permission to publish.

Chapter 1

Michael and Darren

Darren: Walking Up the Steps

I'm being told to accept that I am irredeemably sick. There is no escape; this is it for the rest of my life. This is as grim as it gets.

The forensic psychiatrist appointed by my workplace insurer has determined I am unable to return to work. I am granted permanent invalidity retirement. I've felt the stigma of mental illness for years, but my own judgement is worse. It's hard to accept that my condition is genuine. The psychiatrist's report is a two edged sword, a vindication of sorts; yes, I am legitimately sick, but it is also the final certification of me as a social parasite.

I was diagnosed with severe depression 18 years ago, but my background of depression and anxiety spans 25 years. My darkest days manifest an inability to operate, spending three quarters of the day in bed. I have virtually no social interaction, little or no enjoyment of life and have little interest in self-care. Following the breakdown of my marriage I moved out of the family home. There have been numerous return to work plans that all ended in failure. I have suffered a major heart attack, had triple bypass surgery and lost the sight in one eye.

I never talk suicide; my problems don't seem important enough. A major consideration is what it would do to my kids. I've never had a 'plan.' The closest I have come is thoughts of lining up a tree.

All my energy is devoted to fighting off the enemy, the self-loathing, the self-blaming — lazy, stupid, a failure at everything; dealing with all these on a day to day basis. There is enormous effort involved in making myself presentable to the external world, to my family, helping out at kid's sports, going through the 'show.' When I get home I collapse and the demons come down to pick at me again; vultures on roadkill. To an external observer I'm not doing much. But I'm so tired doing it. Forcing myself to eat, trying to stay alive in an environment of despair, catastrophisation and guilt, with absolutely no energy. I have no legitimate reason for how I am feeling. It turns sad into pathetic.

The impact of my depression continues to take its toll. My psychologist, Anne, is so concerned with my mental state that she interrupts our session and drives me to see my psychiatrist, Dr Don Lawrence. Not long after, Don recommends a period of hospitalisation to try Electroconvulsive Therapy (ECT). Don explains that ECT has led to breakthroughs when all other treatments have proved ineffective. He considers my situation requires significant intervention.

I am admitted into the psychiatric ward and begin ECT, together with counselling and group work. After the first 'treatment' I go to the canteen for breakfast. A woman asks, 'What would you like to eat?' I struggle to answer; my mind is a fog.

Seeing myself in hospital, I realise how low I have sunk. They have taken away all my medications — even the aspirin. I feel the stigma. On the outside I can pretend to be normal, but in here the bricks and mortar and rules show me a different reality. I find this confronting and, in some ways, it makes things harder. Being inside is saying, 'listen, this is serious' and I can't pretend. The temptation is to give in and just be mad, to just not care anymore. The basics of life are so bloody hard anyway — when you take away the pretence of 'I'm OK,' it drains the little bit of energy I did have just to stay alive. After seven sessions with no positive impact, Don and I agree to end the ECT.

In the following two years I continue trying all the traditional forms of treatment; the anti-depressant medication and talk therapy, giving them my best shot. The people treating me are among the best in their field, but after so many years I'm fairly certain these interventions are not going to produce any positive difference. I have tried the full range of treatment options. I don't have anywhere else to go.

Anne suggests I see Michael Masani, a local hypnotherapist. "His approach is different and he's getting good results. You might have more success with his methods," she says. "If you like I can discuss it with Don." Don is supportive and writes a referral.

The idea of meeting with Michael engenders fear on a number of levels. A hypnotherapist; I imagine he might really 'put me under' — whatever that means! I am scared of the unknown, scared of things I can't control. I don't believe I need relaxation, rather I need to work harder. Why should a lazy slob like me be undertaking relaxation? I spend a lot of time in bed already.

Seeing Michael means yet another person to whom I will need to tell my story. I am sick of telling my story, hearing my words over again, simultaneously judging myself for the pathetic state I'm in.

Twelve months later I finally arrange an appointment. The therapy I am about to start is called Private Subconscious-mind Healing (P.S.H.). Who knows what this involves? I could be embarking on some new-age, tree-hugging bullshit — but it is the prospect of losing control that makes me dread this moment more than when I went in for ECT. This is the last throw of the dice, the act of a desperate man out of options.

I walk up the steps to Michael's clinic and knock on the door for my first appointment.

Michael: Becoming a Therapist

I never set out to be a therapist. Serendipity led me here. I qualified as a chartered accountant in July 1969, whereupon I left England to settle in Australia. For several years I worked in Sydney for a multi-national development company. That could have been my meal ticket for life. I was overpaid and over stressed. A plumb job; my friends were envious, but somehow it was not the life for me.

By happy fortune I met upon Walter and Gita Bellin, who were teaching meditation courses in my locality. It was a chance meeting that would change my life. Meditation was the difference for me; within weeks my anxiety reduced and the headaches disappeared into the ether. Several friends I made on the course were experiencing similar benefits.

It was 1980. At that time meditation was on the fringes, generally considered Hippysville. Whenever the subject was mentioned, I would be met with polite smiles and eyes that turned away too quickly. At other times there was outright mockery. I have always cared too much about what other people think of me, a function of my own insecurity. Surprisingly I carried on regardless, doing more training with the Bellins. I was feeling good about myself and more confident than any time I could remember since primary school. Outside the group, I was careful who I talked to, particularly my work colleagues. But it troubled me to lead this double life.

I began training to be a meditation teacher. More good fortune led me to meet a number of wonderful teachers and I learned many different forms of meditation. I found a vocation I felt passionate about. I quit my day job, where by now I was finance director, and threw myself into the new age. Much has transpired in the meantime. Meditation, particularly mindfulness, has become respectable and these days I regularly receive referrals from local GPs and other health professionals. Now into my 70s, I have been practicing and teaching meditation for half my life.

Fortunately, things were not that simple. It was the difficulties I encountered as I began to teach that have made this journey so rich and rewarding. The frustrations and failures sharpened my need to keep learning. The blocks and detours led me in directions I would not otherwise have trod and ultimately to a career I never imagined as a therapist and from there to meet Darren — perhaps my greatest challenge and my greatest teacher.

Not everyone takes to meditation. Some people seem too tense and anxious to even begin to sit still. I was aware from the start how excruciating their attempts were; their inability to tolerate the stillness, often giving up in frustration. I couldn't blame them. These were traditional techniques that had been taught for thousands of years; essential truths, but from a very different time in history. There was no allowance for the stress and change of modern society. Further conflict arose whenever a meditation practice was packaged with certain religious beliefs. I was clear from the start that meditation did not need any such beliefs; the practice and the benefits that followed spoke for themselves. But as I began teaching, I knew that I needed to adapt how I taught the practices to help people relax sufficiently to enter meditation. What I didn't know was how.

In an attempt to find answers, I trained in a number of areas, most notably hypnotherapy and drama. I began to develop the full range of my voice and discovered the therapeutic power of storytelling. I had more certificates on my wall and my library was growing.

My search for answers led me to Frank Wright. He was in town to give a talk about 'analytical hypnotherapy.' Frank explained that he had been practicing hypnotherapy for many years, but found this adaptation far more effective for issues of anxiety and depression. He had got his ideas from a meeting with the Canadian psychiatrist Edgar Barnett[1] while Barnett was on a speaking tour in Sydney.

Gut instinct led me to follow up with Frank and after several more meetings, I committed to doing a period of training with him and his colleague, Greg Brice, at his base in the Blue Mountains. Analytical hypnotherapy was considered so different to traditional hypnotherapy that it underwent a name change and was reborn as P.S.H. therapy, or to give it its full name, 'Private Subconscious-mind Healing.' It featured on national television when Frank was twice interviewed on the Midday Show. Even so, I had no idea then how profoundly P.S.H. therapy would affect my life.

Over the next 15 months, Frank and Greg taught a group of twelve intrepid explorers including myself, the various aspects of P.S.H. therapy. I was able to combine the skills gained from teaching meditation with a new understanding of memory, stress and subconscious communication. The result was an effective, if somewhat raw, individual therapy that dissolved the effects of anxiety.

I know now that anxiety can only be dissolved by means of our autonomic nervous system. P.S.H. promotes a form of unconscious mindfulness, accessing the deeper structures of the brain and mind — in particular the emotional brain and emotional memories. It is a facilitator rather than a fixer, broadening the capacity of our unconscious awareness to resolve deeply buried pains, drawing those hurts into what Stephen Levine calls the 'heart of healing.'[2] Through a combination of trance, story and voice, P.S.H. triggers a cascade of self-healing, self-generating responses that lead to emotional resolution and mental calm.

P.S.H. was the game changer that led to expanding my practice as a meditation teacher and, later down the track, to becoming a full time therapist.

I have been practicing P.S.H. therapy for nearly 30 years. It is essentially a short term therapy, averaging four to six sessions, but can be longer depending on the severity of the condition. The outcomes are good, sometimes amazingly so — evidenced by a regular stream of referrals from past clients and local health professionals. This is a rewarding time in my career, yet I'm still keen to learn more about the workings of the mind and the subconscious. I know that P.S.H. therapy assists healing, I see it on a daily basis, but why and how does this healing take place? Can science explain the unconscious processes of our inner mind? Most pressing of all, I want to know more about the nature of anxiety and depression, the two most common conditions that I see in my clinic room.

Perhaps the seeds to my passion concerning the mind were planted by my elder brother, Peter — himself a Jungian analyst, now retired. His interest in the mind impacted on the younger me more than I realised at the time. When I migrated to Australia, he drove the family, Mum, Dad, myself and my dearest friends, Chris and Tessa to Southampton docks, where the boat was waiting to carry me to the other side of the world. As we hugged goodbye, Peter gave me a gift. It was a book by the famous psychotherapist, Carl Rogers, titled, 'On Becoming a Person.'[3] Peter had written in it, 'to take with you on your journey…' I passed through the gates alone, miniscule beneath the hulk of the great ocean liner and looked back at the tears of my family. I gripped my prized book tighter. Throughout that voyage I found comfort reading its pages, holding tight to the precious connection with the life I had forsaken.

The book left an indelible mark on me. I have a deep appreciation for Rogers and the client centred approach he pioneered. It would be 24 years after I disembarked at Circular Quay to begin my new life that I set up my first practice in Canberra. I had indeed taken Rogers with me 'on my journey.' In the desert outback, seeds can lie dormant for just as long. But when the time is right and the rains come, the desert blooms.

Perceptions have changed a lot since those early days of teaching meditation — an evolution that has taken mindfulness from Hippysville to Hollywood. I am always grateful for the referrals I get from other health professionals, but the day I got a referral from Don Lawrence I admit I was flattered. I knew of Don's reputation as the leading psychiatrist in Canberra and I had met him once at a seminar he was giving to Lifeline counsellors. (I remember it well; it was a seminar on depression.) I am not a psychologist and it is rare for psychiatrists to refer outside of this discipline. I felt my heart swell, though pride is not a recommended attribute for a therapist.

The referral itself was very brief, but I remember staring at it for some time; by implication, this would be an unusual case. I did not know that it would be another twelve months before I finally got to meet Darren. I also did not know just how unusual and challenging the assignment would be.

Healing The Mind That Can't Let Go

Chapter 2

Depression
– No Ordinary Sadness

There are two identical chairs in my clinic room. Darren collapses into one, facing me diagonally across the room and gives a deep sigh, "Aaah dear." He looks out through the windows behind me drinking his coffee, then reclines the chair and pulls a blanket over his outstretched legs. His eyes look dull and his face has dark patches. He has not slept well.

Darren is one of those clients whose condition seems intractable. Middle aged and medium height, he would not normally stand out. His greying head is held slightly to one side; the prominent eyebrows are adjustable, as though looking out from under an awning. Blackened front teeth reveal years of self-neglect. His eyes don't quite meet mine. Instead he looks upward, searching for the auto-cue under the awning, a mannerism that reminds me of the late Bob Hawke.

There are long silences amidst the monotone. I want to finish his sentences, not for his benefit, but for mine. I sense how important it is to Darren that he catches the right words, his own precise phrase. I resist the urge to help and sit with my discomfort. His voice groans, expressionless.

"I feel a sense of futility, a lack of control; I don't believe it will change — the problem is beyond me... The feeling is turbulent... I'm in a fog...."

He hands me a referral from his psychiatrist, Don Lawrence. I received a copy of this referral in the mail over a year ago and I wonder why it took him so long to get here. I make no mention of it, just glad he made it after all. Darren tells me he is an invalid retiree and has suffered major depression for over 18 years. During that period he has spent time in a psychiatric ward, received many forms of psychotherapy, seen dozens of psychologists and psychiatrists, received the full gamut of anti-depressant medications and a period of electric shock therapy. The extended period of depression has affected his physical health. He has suffered a major heart attack, had triple bi-pass surgery and lost the sight in one eye. His partial loss of sight is not directly attributable to depression — just another loss to bear.

Darren's doctors have tried everything they know, but with little effect. There have been occasional periods of modest improvement, but these were short lived and his experience is that nothing really changes. His situation seems hopeless; still here he is and I am amazed at the courage that keeps him trying after 18 years of despair. This is where our story begins.

"There's this rock in the centre of my chest. It's been there for years and it contains all the bad stuff, all my depression." Slowly Darren describes the rock in minute detail, both visually and kinaesthetically. The intimate depiction gives the rock substance, beyond just a feeling of tension. This is more than his imagination. The colouring, the size, the shape, the temperature (cold), the feel (hard and dimpled) and its persistence over time makes it real. It is as though he is this cold, hard, impersonal thing. I note how important the rock seems to Darren; it may well prove meaningful in our therapy.

Darren tells me he would like to feel less restricted, less laboured in his speech, more spontaneous, but that is beyond him. He must edit his words carefully. He needs certainty. This is who he is; as real as the rock.

We talk for a while, then I prepare Darren for meditation. It is voice guided meditation, using story, pacing and vocal modulation to encourage a relaxation response. I explain the central idea of 'witnessing', observing his thoughts and sensations as they arise, but without engaging with them.

"Let them come, let them go, like bits of flotsam; keep coming back to the sound of my voice. Let my voice be the focus, like an anchor; hold it lightly."

Darren protests; "I can't just let go of my thoughts, everything has to be processed, otherwise...otherwise that's just a lazy cop-out."

Darren continues to object and his intensity shocks me.

"Thoughts come unbidden, like spam," I explain. "They are random, 'monkey-mind' stuff. The trick is to avoid clicking on the link."

Darren doesn't buy it. I take a different tack. "Letting thoughts go is not the same as doing nothing, it's not a cop out. You are making a positive decision not to process thoughts. The truth is, not all of our thoughts are worthy of our attention."

I don't realise it yet, but Darren is wrestling with a need for control. One consequence of feeling lazy and stupid for most of his life is that he always feels the need to examine everything in his head, making sure at least he gets the next thing right. I rarely find myself at a loss so early on.

Unexpectedly, Darren relents. "OK then. I'll give it a go," he says without another word of explanation. I don't wait for him to change his mind and continue with a minimum of fuss, no big deal. Just a few words about following my voice, not having to do anything, or make anything happen. Wary at first, he closes his eyes. I begin with mundane descriptions of sufficient interest to keep his attention, while carefully avoiding instructions to do anything — least of all to relax and let go. Such words would raise all his subconscious alarms.

"...feeling the breath a little slower, a little deeper...A good place to start — the breath is always there, always present. We can't live a moment of the day without the need to breathe...an integral part of life...yet mostly we're not even aware that we are breathing... it just happens while we're busy doing other things... Except those times when you've had difficulty breathing, or been underwater for any length of time, then you know how important the next breath is. So if you can, feel each breath now as though it were that next breath. In that real sense, each breath allows life to continue. It's that precious..."

Anxiety is often accompanied by a consuming need for control in our life. Holding our self together, muscles tight, prepared for the worst — a state totally at odds with Darren's attempts to relax and let go. The tension he carries — has seemingly carried for decades — is both an involuntary response to earlier hurt and loss and a defence against future wounds. If he lets his guard down he risks being left vulnerable, defenceless… Darren's need for control is so deep it has never been questioned, never verbalised. His physical and mental contraction is unconscious. Similarly, the letting go response, the very antithesis of anxiety, is autonomic and cannot be summoned by conscious will — however much it may be desired. This is the battle going on inside Darren right now; his need for control pitted against his attempts at letting go; whether to risk vulnerability for the possibility of something he is not even sure will help him.

Head upright, eyes closed, I see tension in his jaw and in his hands curled tight. Even though his eyes are closed, I turn my gaze away. Nobody likes being stared at. We are on a knife-edge. The first critical point in our therapy. If this goes well, he will learn something important about himself. But if Darren's anxiety wins… it will be another failure to add to his growing list. Anything I do might trip the alarms, ramping up contraction and fear. I curse the creaking chair. I want to slow my voice, but not too soon.

"Breathing in new life energy, new life force. Filling your head with light. Breathing the light down into your chest — into that fine delicate tracery of passageways inside your chest — the alveoli — forming a magical gateway for the oxygen to pass into your bloodstream… then imagine streams of light flowing out from your

lungs and heart, branching out and dividing and dividing, out to the far flung galaxies of your body, then spilling out and bathing the cells and tissue.... And there are upwards of 50 trillion cells in our body — an unimaginable number. And every single cell is nourished and nurtured by every breath we take..."

A quick look shows me that Darren's jaw is a little softer, his fingers have loosened, his breath has slowed. Suddenly he moans and shifts position, his arms spread out to his side. It is so tenuous, this stage of the process. He could open his eyes at any moment and lose it. His head — slightly tilted left before, has come back to upright. But his eyes stay closed and he settles once more. I stretch the vowels a little, building a rhythm that increases pitch and volume at the start of the phrase and trails away in lower tones at each finish.

"Fifty trillion points of light, all illuminated by every breath, all interconnected. The complexity, the organisation involved, is staggering... and yet this is just one of hundreds of functions your inner mind performs every moment of every hour of every day of your life. And along with the in breath there's the outbreath — our need to let go of what's past. You can't have one without the other. You can't have the in breath and not the outbreath... and you can't have the outbreath without the in breath. It's all one thing; a cycle of breath, a cycle of life..."

There is no mention of the word relax. I avoid telling Darren to do anything. Just telling him to relax at this early stage could trigger his fear of losing control. It might also cause Darren to make a big effort to relax, ironically putting him back in conscious control. Darren has been on hyper-alert for most of his life, so for him, letting go can feel like losing control. I never use the term resistance, because this is not a conscious choice, the hyper-alert is involuntary and it will take a lot of gentle persuasion for the unconscious to release its grip.

After 20 minutes I gently bring Darren back. He blinks as I roll up the blinds.

"I suppose I am feeling relaxed," he acknowledges begrudgingly.

It is a modest start, something to build on in the coming weeks. On its own, one session like this will soon fade, but with repetition comes the possibility of increasing the length and depth of his relaxation, and touching into that dreamy state of reverie we call trance. And with that comes a slower brain frequency and an opportunity to connect with aspects of the mind normally considered to be unconscious. But I am getting way too far ahead of myself. I can't even be sure he will return next week.

The following week Darren does return — on time. Talking slowly, he describes more of his depression.

"I am tempted to spare the world from me. Look at what I'm imposing on the world and the people around me. An imposition on society. It's not issues based, it's not self-hate — although that's there — it's more an all-encompassing feeling of uselessness. Depression is more a 'lack of' rather than being about anything. How can you work on the immune system if there is no immune system? How can you fix it if it's not there? Often I feel I'm trying to treat the non-existent, trying to fix up things that I can't fix."

His words 'uselessness' and 'imposition' hang in the room.

They are carefully chosen and I am affected. Nothing in his outward appearance quite matches the despair he is describing. He is broken, but there is no physical evidence like a broken leg; no bone fragments jagging through the skin, no tumour marker readouts. As Darren continues, he becomes less clear; talking about a 'lack of' and 'non-existent.' I am struggling to relate.

"This is all loaded on top of how my life has gone... the underlying problems create further problems at an ever increasing velocity and intensity.... I have less and less control.... The outward me is slowing down, almost to a halt... The internal me is working so hard to push through the maze of glue. Inside my head it's never light, it's congealed; I'm grinding it out."

I move back and forth between feelings of compassion one moment, then frustration the next.

"It's my fault — it's my lack of effort, lack of determination, lack of guts. The situation lies with me to make things better. That all feeds into the problem. I don't open the mail, because opening the mail represents the potential for more bad news. I can't cope with more bad news. It's a childish response, but I can't deal with this now."

I want to argue the point, to remind him he still has positive things in his life, to get him to see some light in the darkness, but then he has heard all that before, hasn't he? Instead I listen to how he describes what is going on inside his head. I make encouraging sounds, 'ah huh,' filling in the long gaps while not wanting to interrupt. Darren's descriptions are slow and painfully thought through:

"On bad days I almost want to prove to myself how bad I am... sucked into the self-pity, the anger against myself. A self-loathing vortex... Self-harm doesn't have to be physical... Occasionally life plays out the self-criticism. I'm doing things that prove my internal talk correct."

How depressing depression is. I note the tightness in my chest and make a conscious choice to listen with compassionate ears. I remember one of my teachers saying, 'healing begins when we are valued enough to be listened to, to be understood, or at least have someone try to understand us.'

Depression is hard to understand. How can we identify with such feelings as, being in a fog, a maze of glue? When people we love say they cannot face the day, continuously breaking down in tears, how are we to respond? More baffling still are times when the simplest tasks appear overwhelming, when opening the mail or answering the phone is torture and when going back to bed is the only solace. Most tragic of all, when thoughts are suicidal, 'I feel the temptation to spare the world from me,' or 'you'll be better off without me.' How can we possibly relate to this ultimate travesty? None of it makes sense; there is nothing else comparable. Unless you have been there yourself.

Darren continues, "I'm too proud to let people know how things are. I'm reluctant to engage with the outside world; I want to hide myself away and fix myself up, but that doesn't work... I avoid situations where I get asked, 'how are you?' 'What have you been up to?' 'Where are you working?' All those questions are so loaded for me. People won't judge, or maybe they will, I don't know; I have these overriding feelings of shame, embarrassment and humiliation. It takes a degree of bravery to engage with the outside world. People who give advice don't realise how difficult it is." The actor, author and comedian Steven Fry has been there and he makes this heartfelt plea:

> "If you know someone who is depressed, please resolve never to ask them, 'why'? Try to understand the blackness, lethargy, hopelessness and loneliness they're going through. Be there for them when they come through the other side. It's hard to be a friend to someone who's depressed, but it is one of the kindest, noblest, and best things you will ever do."[4]

In recent times we have seen a number of people in public life talk about their experience of depression. This is a very brave and important thing to do. Not just television personalities and comedians, but army chiefs, cabinet ministers — even an Aussie prime minister, top selling authors, leading barristers, football heroes and test cricketers; people who, by any standard are leading highly successful lives. Because of their courage we learn something important about depression. This is no ordinary sadness; there is no amount of winning and no amount of success in life that can take away this dreadful state. It does not help to tell these people, 'look at how brilliant you are and see the things you've achieved!' Because rather than feel cheered by such comments, it may only add to the hopelessness. Depression does not respect position or status; we are all potentially vulnerable.

There is a road to depression, a road to hell. Not the only road, but the one most travelled. More like a goat track really; overgrown and full of potholes. It's called anxiety. Darren's anxiety is crippling; it is diminishing his confidence, eroding his self-worth and changing his personality. His natural joy and sparkle have long gone. It will be some time before Darren shares details of his past with me, so I cannot yet know what has caused his anxiety, but it is unmistakably there in his manner and his words, in his voice and in the eyes that rarely meet mine. There are shades of humiliation and shame in his attempts to shield himself from public interaction. His slow ponderous voice and long pauses in conversation show how careful he is with every utterance, lest he be misunderstood or misrepresented, a defence against criticism and judgement. While these are aspects of anxiety, I am also aware of something different; talk of 'fog' and 'treacle,' of an 'all-encompassing feeling of uselessness and imposition.' These are descriptors of his depression. Darren alternately displays symptoms of both anxiety and depression and he is, unknowingly, describing the inter-relationship between the two.

Darren's condition is characterised by an inability to move, think and function as he would wish. It is like buffering on slow speed internet. He talks repeatedly of depression in the same way:

"My brain feels like treacle, all gluggy. It isn't an inability to operate entirely, but it is slow and confused; everything takes great effort — just the amount of sheer effort."

Darren knows he has the competence to perform most tasks. He is not paralysed. There is nothing physically wrong. Not that he can see. Yet even simple tasks seem mountainous. He is ashamed when basic parenting duties are beyond him. Worse still is how this crippling condition affects his mood, there is no joy, no light — just an unrelenting world of grey. A common factor in the diagnosis of depression is the inability to feel joy — even when hearing good news, or experiencing a happy event.

Curiously Darren tells me he does not feel sadness either, which runs counter to the common perception of depression. "Feeling sad is OK — feeling nothin' is depression," he says. This is possibly an extreme version of the condition; depression expresses itself in various ways. Other clients describe a 'heavy sadness' that weighs down on their chest and tummy. Darren tells me he wishes he could feel sadness — "that would be infinitely better than what I am experiencing." His depression is not a feeling or emotion as such. Certainly he does describe having feelings at times; he talks of shame and self-loathing, but he talks more tellingly of emptiness, a lack of, the non-existent. It is as though there are feelings on the periphery of his experience, emotional satellites orbiting a central black hole.

You might think that not feeling sadness or anger is a good thing; a kind of psychic defence. Not so; this is a hellish void, lacking the most basic humanity, accompanied by a lack of energy, motivation and desire. Far from being a defence, Darren's emptiness is more like a black parasite slowly devouring him from the inside. Listening to his descriptions of depression, what strikes me is that it does indeed seem like a semi paralysis; one that is affecting him physically, mentally and emotionally.

"The internal me is drowning, it's more and more difficult to churn through the treacle; it's getting thicker and thicker, more and more stuff coming in. I can't process it; everything is looping back in, I can't make decisions, I can't achieve outputs, everything is coming in and nothing is going out. Opening the mail is more input. Everything I try to do increases the level. Shovelling more into the melting pot; the turbine has to work harder and harder…" Darren's reality is grim, unlike any other human experience.

He goes on, "…how I move, how I talk, everything I do, life gets narrower; less external contact. I progress from world — to family — to house — to coffin. All this in an environment of treacle-fog. Each step becomes more dark and viscous. It doesn't make sense, I can't see through it to find out what's going on. I'm getting more and more tired, unable to motivate myself. I'm spending more time in bed — that's the step between house and coffin."

Life has no comfort, no meaning. It is only to be endured. A meaningless emptiness; as though 'non-feeling' equates to 'non-being.' Feelings are at the core of our being — they shape our sense of self from the time we are born when all communication is through sensation and feeling. As we grow, communication develops and we learn language and cognition; but our core self remains centred on how we feel about ourselves, our work, our achievements, our status, and how we feel in relation to our family and loved ones. When we become clinically depressed we cease, in varying degrees, to feel in the same way and this causes a chasm to open where our sense of self once was. We have lost certain fundamentals of aliveness — something so innate we never knew what it was we had until it has gone. This is the devastating nature of depression. It is beyond despair, beyond feeling; it is the Black Dog and it has been around for a while. Here is a description from 2,000 years ago:

> 'No company's more hateful than your own
> You dodge and give yourself the slip; you seek
> In bed or in your cups from care to sneak.
> In vain: the black dog follows you and hangs
> Close on your flying skirts with hungry fangs'.
> Horace (65-8BC)[5]

The black dog has haunted Darren for so long, I wonder can he seriously believe things will change? Yet he keeps turning up. Some weeks Darren comes in feeling 'shocking.' I try to hide my disappointment. But he ups the ante, telling me he is feeling even worse than before. This is not good. Am I doing something wrong? Am I causing him more suffering? I am surprised that he still turns up. My prime edict, 'first, do no harm' is glowing, giant and red. I go over our recent sessions to look for clues as to what might be happening. My approach has been similar to how I am with most cases of depression and anxiety. Occasionally a session can stir up old feelings. It is a temporary state that I know will soon pass. The next session will help move the process on; sometimes movement happens during sleep and the person wakes the next day feeling lighter. This is different, not what I am used to. Darren seems mired.

We chat for a while. A few weeks ago he seemed to be going OK. I surprise myself with sudden boldness,

"Do you want to continue?"

His reply stuns me, "Shit, yeah. I might be feeling worse, but you gotta understand any change is better than none." Then he adds for good measure, "I don't know if this stuff will work, but the worst thing for me is to experience no change at all. I need to feel movement; I'm trying hard to find any glimmer of light. I didn't come here for a good time."

I had, of course, hoped Darren would continue, but facing the choice seemed an important step for him to take. His courage and resolve are impressive, but he dismisses this saying, "I don't have any choice". While somewhat reassured, I know that we will need to make more progress soon. I tell him I would like to lengthen the meditations.

Despite everything, Darren *is* having brief moments of respite and a taste of something different. His attitude has changed; the fear of losing control has gone and there is no more talk of 'tree hugging bullshit.' His life outside the clinic room might not have changed, but he actually looks forward to these sessions, declaring on one occasion, "It's time out from the frenzy in my head — like a holiday!"

As I lead each meditation, my voice becomes my greatest asset.

It has evolved over years of teaching people to meditate. I don't try to change how I speak, or physically make it sound different, yet I am hearing a broader range of tones, aware of playing with the timing, pitch and modulation, bringing life to the stories, while simultaneously coaxing Darren into a deeper meditative trance.

Our conversations are evolving. At first, we were confined to the usual discussion of how his life was going. Now we are finding a wider discourse, taking in a range of subjects. I am searching for things he used to like doing before he became depressed. There are surprising areas of common ground. We both had a love of horse racing in the past. Neither of us have looked at a form guide for over 20 years, but we chat happily about the horses, trainers and jockeys that were around in the 70s and 80s. It is an unexpected pleasure for both of us. A little off topic, perhaps, but seeing Darren smile again tells me this is OK therapy. We are closer, less formal. These conversations are building more understanding and trust between us.

Some weeks the churn inside his head is louder and meditation is difficult, but most of the time Darren is able to relax more easily and deeply. At times he is so deep he does not even hear my voice. The effect lasts a few hours before he is thrust back into the treacle pit and the rock in his heart. Still, for these brief periods of time, there are inklings of a different experience emerging.

Chapter 3

A Complicating Factor

It is one of those perfect Sunday mornings in the nation's capital; the lake spotted with rowing crews, while autumn colours dance in their wake. The National Library and the High Court pose proudly in the low angled sunlight, happily playing backdrop to a thousand holiday snaps. People everywhere are preparing for a day of fun and adventure. But not me.

I have enrolled in a one day workshop for volunteer telephone counsellors — the subject, depression. As I take my seat in the dreary lecture hall, I ponder on the choices we make; 15 Lifeline counsellors preparing to spend the day shut inside a dusty, neon lit room, discussing the saddest of all human afflictions.

Today's presenter is a psychiatrist, who introduces himself as Dr Don Lawrence. He has with him a large number of reference books. I'm impressed, he is taking us seriously. Why wouldn't he? Well, perhaps because we are not psychology students, just volunteers. But Don is not interested in status. Greying hair and past middle age, he talks with the authority that comes from a lifetime of treating the mentally ill, but what is also clear from the start is that he talks without ego. The work has not soured on him and I realise that his very presence here today — for he is volunteering his time — speaks to his humanity, as someone who cares.

By lunchtime I have become engrossed in Don's stories and forgotten the sunshine and the outside world. How wise I was to choose to be here! Even so, I could not tell how pivotal this day would be for me, or how it would become a beacon amongst my memories for a long time. Many years later I received a letter from Dr Lawrence that had another significant impact on me. It was the referral to treat Darren for major depression and anxiety.

My first real encounters with depression were while working as a telephone counsellor for Lifeline Canberra. The training we were given was based on the work of psychologist Carl Rogers. It was the same Carl Rogers whose writing my brother had introduced me to all those years ago at Southampton Docks, as I tearfully farewelled family and friends before departing for Australia. Rogers was a pioneer of 'Person-Centred Therapy,' a non-directive approach that acknowledged the self-healing and self-actualising resources within each of us. He talked of the need for the therapist to display empathy and 'unconditional positive regard' for the client. It was a radical move away from the traditional model of the therapist as the 'expert' who, from some vaunted status of super-hero, would *fix* the client's problem behaviours and aberrant thoughts. Instead, here was a model that placed the therapist in a more human role, where the development of a caring relationship between her/him and the client was the first priority. This was an approach that would serve and nurture the growing edge of both client and therapist. It was a model of therapy to which I felt intuitively drawn.

After the usual period of training, I was gradually exposed to live calls, with a supervisor listening in. I prepared to hear difficult, perhaps desperate stories, alert for signs of despair and possible self-harm. At first I would over-identify with a caller, tempted to 'fix' their problems, freely giving my advice whether or not it was asked for. My supervisor gently pointed out this was not as helpful as I had imagined. Despite the excellent training I had received, despite reading Carl Rogers cover to cover and despite all the hours spent with my many meditation teachers, it took me a while to feel comfortable with the idea of 'just being with' someone in pain. I had to let go of the extraordinary conceit that I was their fixer. I learned the value of 'active listening' to someone in distress — to quote Steven Levine, 'not grasping to their pain, but letting it float in compassion and care.'[6] I remember surprising moments when I could hear relief in the caller's voice, never quite sure how that had occurred. Those five years spent with Lifeline in the 1990s were invaluable for me personally and as preparation to becoming a psychotherapist.

The mystery of what causes depression is as old as time. We are 2,000 years on from Horace and the black dog still hangs to our skirts. We have lists of symptoms, such as feeling intense sadness, despair, inability to feel any enjoyment in life, but nowhere in the authoritative texts do we find agreement as to the cause of this terrible distress, or why it is happening. The dictionary tells us depression is a 'mood disorder,' but that again is a symptom. There is a yawning gap in our understanding of depression and this ignorance adds to the social stigma around mental illness.

Given that symptoms are all we have to go on, it is no surprise to find that mainstream treatment for depression is entirely symptom driven. No surprise, either, to find that these current treatments are not as effective as we would wish. While ever we confuse the symptoms for the malady, we risk derailing the pursuit of a more effective therapy and fail to provide better community understanding of mental illness. Lack of understanding can have unfortunate consequences. A desire to help will sometimes end up having the opposite effect. Recently Darren was told, "Look, everybody has down days. You've just got to get on with life." In that person's understanding, depression is just about having 'down days.' Darren didn't have the strength to argue. Comments like, 'pull your socks up,' or 'get over it' only make matters worse. They are born out of ignorance. Suggestions to make-pretend, or 'fake it till you make it' were, to quote Darren, 'like a band aid without adhesive.' Depression is not just an accumulation of bad habits.

Even a kinder approach can miss the point. Strategies that encourage more positive self-talk and self-love may appear the perfect antidote to counter disparaging self-talk. But what if there are deeper causes driving the self-hate and negative attitudes? More self-love and positive self-talk are certainly desirable qualities, but such affirmations were of little help to Darren and my sense is that deeper emotional wounds need to be addressed.

The constant lethargy and despair are made worse, if that were possible, because he cannot understand why it is happening. He assumes it is on account of his own weakness. He feels the stigma, he feels at fault for not being stronger and berates himself for his apparent laziness and his oh-so-many failings. A range of talk therapies over the years has failed to bring about any significant change and Darren assumes this, too, is his failure. Another to add to his growing list and seized upon by his inner critic as further proof of him being useless and worthless. Not understanding the condition adds to the suffering, reinforces the social stigma and lessens our chances of collectively finding a more effective therapy.

Working with depressed and anxious clients over many years has shown me that, invariably, anxiety precedes depression. Anxiety always comes first and it is this sequence that provides a clue to the causal link. Not everyone who has anxiety will become depressed, but people with depression always have levels of anxiety. Does that mean anxiety causes depression? I am careful not to equate correlation with causation, nevertheless this looks more than coincidence. For years I puzzled over how the two were related. Then one day, quite unexpectedly, I got it.

I was listening to Professor Russell Meares giving a talk about dissociation, a pathological state commonly found in people with Borderline Personality Disorder.[7] Someone suffering from dissociation will commonly feel disconnected from their sensory experience and their sense of self. Meares has worked with this most difficult condition for many years and written extensively on the subject. Halfway through his talk, I was busily scribbling down notes when I swear I had a pie-in-the-face moment.

Meares was proposing that dissociation was not a psychological avoidance or defence, as was commonly thought. Rather, dissociation was a disorganisation of the cerebral function due to overwhelming trauma. I hasten to add dissociation is different to depression, although the two often co-exist. Regardless, the thought of a systemic collapse made me realise — that is exactly what depression is! The unrelenting torment of anxiety overloads our nervous system, leading to a mental collapse and the subsequent symptoms of emptiness and exhaustion. All of a sudden I can better understand Darren's description of his mental state, 'I'm pushing through glue; everything is so hard.' Although I have never experienced depression, when I worked as a finance executive, I did experience moments of extreme anxiety where it felt as if my head would explode. I knew firsthand something of the sheer force being exerted on the brain at those times and I have since heard similar descriptions in the clinic room. I thought about all the clients I had known with depression and in every case the idea of systemic collapse in the face of severe anxiety was a perfect fit.

The feelings that accompany anxiety can become so destructive that they start to affect the functioning of the brain. Anxiety is serious. An inner tyrant that demands our hyper-vigilance, replays past traumas, the 'what ifs', the 'if onlys,' the dreadful grief — while conjuring up endless catastrophic scenarios into the future. There is little respite, even at night, placing enormous strain on our nervous system. There are corresponding corrosive effects on our endocrine system (stress hormones elbowing out our endorphins, the would-be harbingers of healing), our muscular-skeletal system (pulled out of shape by chronically tense muscles) and our digestive system (so much fear we want to vomit). Anxiety clouds our thinking and impairs our memory and decision making ability. It disrupts sleep patterns, leaving us desperately tired. This further depletes our immune system and erodes our mental resilience. I cannot think of a more dramatic example of mind/body connection.

Darren's experience fits my working theory perfectly. He acknowledges his depression and many times has described his own feelings of collapse. Yet strangely he does not recognise any pre-existing anxiety, telling me, "I wouldn't say I was anxious." This is despite the fact he has several psychiatrists' reports describing his condition as 'major depression and anxiety.' I do not try to persuade him otherwise, but I am curious. Why would he not recognise his own anxiety when it seems obvious to others? As things transpire, Darren will shortly begin to realise the extent to which anxiety is gripping him.

Archimedes is said to have had an 'aha' moment while lying in his bath one day — something about the weight of water displaced by his body. He was so taken by his sudden flash of insight that he leapt up from his bath and ran down the street, oblivious to his lack of cover, shouting 'Eureka!' to the astonishment of bystanders. Now this was unusual behaviour, even for ancient Greece. Truth, or urban myth, we may never know, but as a teenager I just thought he was weird. However that story stuck in my mind and helped me remember an important principle of physics that changed the world forever. It led to the building of enormous steel ships that could carry huge tonnages without sinking.

It is strange to think that an academic physicist would discover his moment of genius in the bath. Stranger still that he would be so overcome by feelings of wonder that he would lose all self-consciousness in his moment of elation. Just as well it was ancient Greece and not the middle of a Canberra winter! The story highlights the feeling engendered by discovering the answer to a riddle, or a long pondered puzzle. It is a special form of joy — euphoria in Archimedes' case. We all have our Archimedes moments that come in times of quiet reflection, taking a bath, or walking in nature, when our synapses fire in a different orbit. Such occasions nurture our creativity and wellbeing. Hearing Professor Meares' talk was such an Archimedes moment for me: it forever changed my view of depression.

I began to imagine depression as analogous to a blown fuse, leading to the collapse of an electrical circuit. This idea grew to include a network of circuits and many blown fuses. The use of analogies can be helpful in understanding complex issues. It reminds me of an old fashioned phrase, heard commonly in my childhood, of having a 'nervous breakdown.' The image of a blown fuse in an overcharged electrical circuit may be over-simplifying the unfathomable intricacies of the human brain;

nevertheless it is a helpful picture that enables me to get my head around a complex phenomenon. It is useful, too, to remind myself these fuses cannot be reset by throwing the switch to positive thinking, telling ourselves to be happy. The circuitry is overloaded and this needs to be attended to as a matter of priority. Our life force is compromised and the lights have gone out. A short while later I came across an interesting piece of research regarding the neuroscience of depression that made me realise how pertinent the fuse analogy was.

Eric Nestler, MD, PhD, Professor of Neuroscience and Director of the Friedman Brain Institute at Mount Sinai, talks not of fuses, but of complex sets of genes that operate across different areas of the brain.[8] Nestler explains how the expression of these genes becomes altered in depression. (Epigenetics tells us that genes can either be on or off — just like fuses.) According to Nestler, "Depression is a circuit-level disorder and needs to be understood and treated at that level." I agree, but the problem is not with the genes themselves. The issue is, why did the expression of the genes become altered? What power surge caused them to switch off? None other than the crushing effects of anxiety.

For years we have talked of anxiety and depression in the same breath without knowing how the two were connected. Now I have a clearer understanding of the way they are linked. Suddenly it is clear to me that depression is a brain malfunction — not the chemical imbalance previously thought, but a systemic breakdown. This breakdown, or 'circuit level disorder' is for the most part, the result of enormous forces placed on our brain and nervous system by anxiety and the factors that make up anxiety, namely trauma and deep emotional conflict. Any cure for depression must include a way to dissolve the painful feelings that form the essence of anxiety.

This understanding fits well with the work Darren and I are doing, focusing on helping him relax deeply, so that, as the letting go response kicks in, the pressure eases on his mental circuitry. Guided by my voice, he is able to meditate deeply for periods of 40 minutes at a time. The peace he experiences brings something new — a sense of hope. As he put it on one occasion, "Ah, this is how life's meant to be."

So why has this understanding of depression not been recognised before? It seems simple enough — surely others would have seen the same thing? Many have. Nevertheless, as time passes, the absence of any official word has become a silent scream through psychology's lecture halls. There is a feeling of a forlorn meandering among those in charge of the curriculum. Has psychology lost its way? Sadly, when it comes to depression and anxiety, it appears so and it is not hard to understand why this has been the case. According to Dr Genevieve Rayner, research fellow in Clinical Neuropsychology at the Melbourne School of Psychological Studies, anxiety is often excluded from research studies on depression, because it is considered 'a complicating factor.'[9] Rayner considers this unfortunate and so do I. Research is being led up a blind alley. In the world of computers this is known as GIGO — garbage in, garbage out. False assumptions result in false conclusions. But there is an additional explanation for psychology's strange loss of voice.

Depression is caused by the physical effects of anxiety — the destructive effects that are wrought over time by highly-charged, painful emotions. As a therapist, I see anxiety as the collective experience, conscious and unconscious, of all our unprocessed emotions; terror, grief, rage, loneliness, betrayal, abandonment, shame and self-loathing, to name but some. These are the raw emotions that represent most of human suffering. We try many ways to defend ourselves against feeling the pain, but their effects seep into the tissues of our body and drive the relentless churning inside our head. Emotions are front and centre in our experience of anxiety and therefore depression.

The truth is, our society has difficulty with emotions. Emotions carry associations: worse than painful, there are shades of weakness, irrationality, loss of control, lots of tears and mucous. Consequently, our whole culture would prefer not to deal with emotions, so when it comes to anxiety and depression we have turned a collective blind eye to the obvious, blithely declaring 'I see no ships!' Equally, there is a desire to keep feelings out of any respectable scientific, psychological or dinner table discussion; feelings are not logical — they get very messy and don't follow the rules. This makes things especially awkward when it comes to understanding depression and anxiety, whose entire fabric is woven through with emotion. Like it or not, emotions are core to our fundamental human experience; indeed to our very survival. (Imagine how long you would survive without any fear instinct.)

Emotions are the most wonderful feature of being alive; they are also the most challenging. When feelings are too painful for us to process, they become the basis of anxiety.

Emotions are not irrational and neither are they are rational, they are emotional. Their language is universal, telling us something important about our environment and ourselves, yet for many of us, acknowledging our feelings is never easy and often not encouraged. When our feelings are not treated seriously by others or by ourselves, the result is a communication breakdown; unacknowledged feelings cannot be processed and remain raw inside us. One aspect of good therapy can be seen as a sanctuary where real communication can occur, where we can feel heard and not judged and where feelings can be expressed, processed and let go.

When a client shows emotion in the clinic room I am immediately aware of their truth. Instantaneously I react by feeling a small fraction of what it is they are feeling. There is no cover up, no spin. It is an honour to be let into to their inner world. I try to meet them there. That is where the healing is, in the shared human-ness of the moment, granting emotions passage.

Emotions may not be scientific, nor rational, but they are the very stuff of life from which spring our thoughts, attitudes and behaviour. Emotions come and then go. Mostly. Difficulties arise when painful feelings get caught in a loop that sees them return again and again. This unending re-presentation of negative affect, whether conscious or unconscious, is what we call anxiety and can be the precursor to depression. A major function of therapy is to diffuse this emotional loop and to restore cohesion to our troubled mind. But to achieve this requires us to acknowledge the primacy of our feelings and visceral responses. It is our internal feeling milieu that shapes and colours our thought patterns and behaviour — not vice versa. And that is precisely where it has all come undone.

Healing The Mind That Can't Let Go

Chapter 4

Don't Mention the Feelings

Over the last hundred years, mainstream therapy, keen to fit in with the prevailing cultural norms, has demonstrated an almost comical avoidance of feelings. Behavioural therapy (BT) was first touted in the 1920s and dominated psychological discourse for many years, culminating in the 1960s and 1970s. Roughly stated, BT held that the cause of our problems was found in some variation of aberrant behaviour. Therefore, change the behaviour and we solve the problem. Simple! There was no acknowledgement of self, or values, no reference to meaning and certainly no mention of feelings — this was an all-mechanical, robotic version of humanity. In the words of the philosopher and writer Ken Wilber, it was 'flat-land' — with no depth and no meaning.[10]

The theory was founded by John B. Watson and later championed by the equally infamous B.F. Skinner. It appears Watson based his ideas on Pavlov's famous 'conditioned response' effect, observed while feeding his dogs. These days he would be seen as largely disconnected from his own feelings, a psychological state that mirrored his therapy and that had no qualms about conducting vivisection experiments in order to 'prove' his theories. His dehumanising view of the world was eagerly adopted and reigned supreme for over 40 years, a soulless reductionism that still reverberates around psychology's lecture halls. Watson's ideas flourished because of the times. Psychology was new, trying to establish itself as a respectable 'science' and no respectable science could afford to be seen dabbling in something as ephemeral and insubstantial as feelings.

Finally it was realised that behaviour therapy wasn't working too well. The old guard clung to their old ways as they do, even in the face of evident failure. Progress was funeral by funeral, to paraphrase Max Planck.[11] Behaviour therapy was laid to rest, only to be replaced by cognitive behaviour therapy (CBT). Sticking to the mantra 'don't mention the feelings,' CBT declared the problem to be faulty thinking, which in turn gave rise to unhelpful behaviour. With CBT, the instructions were to change our cognition — our patterns of thinking — and in so doing, we would feel better and the problem would be solved. Rather than acknowledge our hurts, grief and terror as the *generator of our recurring thoughts*, CBT reverses the order and claims we can feel better as a consequence of changing our patterns of thinking. This 'sports coach' approach may be great to whip up morale for the grand final next weekend; however as a therapy for depression and anxiety it simply belies the power of our emotions. Another 40 years on and CBT is still the 'gold standard' approach to anxiety and depression. Combined, that's nearly a century of Fawlty-esque conspiracies, where any mention of feelings is strictly verboten.

Do you think I am exaggerating? Sounds like hyperbole? Here are the views of two leading authorities in modern neuroscience. Firstly, Professor Emeritus of Psychobiology at Bowling Green State University, Jack Panksepp:

> "The cognitive revolution, like radical neuro-behaviourism, intentionally sought to put emotions out of sight and out of mind. Now cognitive science must re-learn that ancient emotional systems have a power that is quite independent of neocortical cognitive processes."[12]

Secondly, neuroscientist, psychotherapist, author and faculty member of the University of California's David Geffen School of Medicine, Dr Allan Schore:

> "The brain, the body and the unconscious were placed in an opaque 'black box' that was not to be opened. In psychoanalysis, drives and motivational states were downgraded and relegated to the realm of metapsychology. And so were emotions, which Skinner said were beyond the pale of scientific investigation."[13]

This is not to say CBT is all wrong. There are thousands of caring psychologists using CBT and time spent with a caring therapist is the most important determinant for a successful outcome, regardless of the modality involved. A great many people have found CBT helpful in developing strategies to better manage their discomfort. There are parts of this approach that are totally valid — but that is my point, a partial truth can sound convincing until you know what has been excluded. Far from a full picture, there are essential aspects of what it means to be human that have been cast aside, or relegated in importance, because those elements are too difficult to measure, define, or control. And sometimes because they are too awkward and too painful to sit with. The empty chair that sits at depression's bedside represents those human qualities that have been subordinated for so long. These unacknowledged feelings and emotions form the core of anxiety and depression. Rather than facing up to the emotional pain, CBT turns its attention to the subsequent avoidance behaviour and warped thought processes. In effect, CBT is telling people, 'Ah, it's the limp that's the problem. Try walking with an even gait.'

Years of avoidance and alienation have not seen our emotional pain diminish — just the opposite. By common agreement we are witness to an ever increasing incidence of anxiety and depression; in part the bitter harvest from years of denial. Now, in our dissociation, we barely recognise the nature of the problem. We can't explain it and our impotent response is some combination of medicate, sedate and question why we have a *cognitive* deficit.

Nevertheless, the times they are a-changing. Advances in neuroscience are revolutionising our understanding of mental health, and foremost among these new discoveries is an appreciation of how emotions arise and are processed through the brain and the body. What was once 'beyond the pale of scientific enquiry' has become the biggest talking point in neuroscience and the subject of a whole new branch of science known as 'affective neuroscience.' (The word 'affect' is used to describe the collective sum of feelings, emotions and visceral bodily responses.) It is hard to overstate the importance of this development. One of the leaders in this new field of endeavour is the aforementioned neuroscientist, psychotherapist and author, Dr Allan Schore. His new book has just arrived by mail — the hardcover version, something to treasure. I am eager to hear what he has to say.

Schore's introduction sets a high bar, describing the discoveries in neuroscience that have taken place in the last few years as a paradigm shift, 'altering the entire field of mental health, including psychotherapy.'[14] Our feelings, shunned and shamed for so long, are now front and foremost in modern neuroscience. How wonderful! For years my colleagues and I have sought to explain a therapy that focuses on feelings and the unconscious. Now here is a whole body of scientific evidence that is creating tectonic quakes in the way we understand ourselves and that has ramifications for years of future therapy.

The central theme of his book is the power and influence of our feelings and emotions. Schore provides the evidence for what has become known as the 'primacy of feelings,' turning 100 years of psychotherapy on its head. Emotions have primacy in a number of ways. They arise without effort or invitation, effectively invading us through a whole of body response, capturing us in a microsecond. Cognition, in comparison, is a more subdued affair — it is self-directed and we must often work hard to reach an understanding, or a conclusion to our thinking.

Schore points to another important aspect: speed. Emotions get there first. They arise much faster than the time it takes to think. Long before we can register a threat in our environment — say a tiger emerging from the forest — our emotions have triggered autonomic responses and actions that assist our survival and help us gain advantage in the dangerous jungle of life. We can run away, or we can fight, or we can freeze. The choice is non-cognitive, non-negotiable — we don't have time to debate. The speed of reaction can mean the difference between life and death. This is how we have evolved. Importantly, this is *why* we have evolved and not joined the growing ranks of the extinct. We have our emotions to thank for the fact that we have survived. So if, in our clever, rational ways, we continue relegating the importance of emotions in our motivations and psychology then, one way or another, we may end up risking our continued presence on the planet.

Turning his attention to therapy, Schore reveals insight into how our brains react in moments of trust and care between two people. It was always considered that the experience of such a precious moment could not be observed or measured and most certainly lay beyond the pale of scientific observation. Not so anymore. Schore describes a video of brain scans taken simultaneously of therapist and client where the neuronal activity matches and corresponds with the felt experiences of the two individuals. These scans show the two brains aligning, synchronising and responding to each other, co-ordinating in a non-verbal communication. For the first time we are now able to witness this phenomenon as it occurs in our brains; the neurological correlate of being 'in tune' with another living being.

In an earlier book by Thomas Verny, titled *Pre-parenting*, we have this wonderful reference to Schore's work as it applies to the mother-child relationship:

> "Synthesizing a vast amount of research, neuroscientist Allan N. Schore ... has shown that during the first two years of life, the maturation of the brain is controlled by interaction with the caregiver. Through this intimate relationship, both subtle in nature and precise in timing, the baby's brain is literally tuned by the caregiver's brain to produce the correct neurotransmitter and hormones in appropriate sequence; this entrainment or patterning, determines the baby's brain architecture in a permanent and powerful way..."[15]

Professor Russell Meares, who developed the widely used psychotherapy model, *The Conversational Method*, based much of his work on the minutiae of mother/infant interactions, placing emphasis on their proto conversations and play. He recognised in these interactions the fundamentals for growth and development of the infant's mind and his/her sense of security in the world. Meares contends that good therapy must learn from and, in certain ways, be analogous to these initial experiences of relationship.[16] Therapy requires a special type of nurturing relationship where feelings-based conversations encourage and stimulate an 'entrainment or patterning' of growth and healing.

Schore's 'paradigm shift' is taking the therapeutic focus away from conscious cognition and toward unconscious affect; away from Cognitive Behaviour Therapy and toward Mindfulness, P.S.H. and a range of right brain dominant therapies. He writes:

> "Neuroscience is transitioning from studies of left brain, language-based cognitive processes and voluntary motor functions, to studies of the embodied functions of the right-lateralised emotion-processing limbic system and the stress regulating hypothalamic-pituitary-adrenal (HPA) axis. In addition to the shift from the left to the right brain, researchers are also moving down from the central nervous system (CNS) to the autonomic nervous system (ANS)."[17]

The last part of the quote is pertinent because while the CNS deals with conscious actions and responses, the ANS deals with our unconscious bodily reactions, arousal and relaxation — 'autonomic' meaning involuntary. The focus is not just on emotions, but on *unconscious emotions*. Our unconscious mind, Sigmund Freud's giant contribution to our knowledge of ourselves, is re-emerging as central to our understanding of anxiety and depression.

It was 1995 when I first heard Frank Wright explain the basics of P.S.H. therapy, declaring, "The problem is a feeling." That same year he was invited to speak on national TV, where he explained, "We are disturbed by painful feelings within the subconscious and the resolution to these disturbances lies in the subconscious. We do not need to know what events caused those disturbances; the subconscious is more concerned with current feelings than past events." These ideas were surprisingly well received by the viewing audience at the time and Frank was invited back for a second interview. It was, as they say, an idea whose time had come.

Frank Wright and Greg Brice developed these principles over several years. With hundreds of successful case studies between them, they knew they could help people with anxiety. Both Frank and Greg were trained hypnotherapists and were used to working with the subconscious mind — but the exclusive focus on feelings was new and the paradoxical idea of unconscious feelings was transformational. P.S.H. therapy was born before the terms 'affective neuroscience' and 'unconscious affect' were even coined. It prophetically encapsulated the yet to be discovered neuroscience. Furthermore, it presented an elegant solution to the problem of how to heal traumas and emotional wounds that in many cases were heavily defended and consigned to the depths of the unconscious, there to be avoided at all costs.

The long search to understand the cause and nature of depression has been sabotaged by an earlier mindset that 'intentionally sought to put emotions out of sight and out of mind.' We have been looking through the pack for a joker that was discarded before we started. Of course, there have been various attempts to feign a joker; to build a case for another explanation where feelings are not needed. Some of these 'alternative causes' persist in people's minds — despite the fact that close inspection reveals they don't stack up. Their lingering presence is the fig leaf covering our phobic response to emotions. It is time for some myth-busting.

For many years it was thought that depression was caused by a chemical imbalance. The elevation of serotonin in the brain that was thought to result from taking medications such as Prozac and Zoloft, can indeed make some people feel better. For this reason it was thought that the cause of depression must be an insufficient level of serotonin. This theory is subject to considerable doubt these days. For one thing, these antidepressants are only effective half the time. There is the awkward problem of knowing how much serotonin is ideal and the inherent difficulties in measuring the levels present in a living brain. A 2013 study by the University of Maryland suggests depression is not so much about insufficient serotonin, but more to do with a disturbance in the ability of brain cells to communicate with each other.[18] We are left wondering what caused the disturbance.

Genes are a convenient suspect in our search for cause. In the absence of anything physically obvious, like a broken bone or an infection, it can be tempting to imagine there is a gene responsible for whether or not we become depressed. However, evidence of an association between genes and depression is not conclusive. According to the US National Institutes of Health, depression doesn't have a clear pattern of genetic inheritance.

At most, certain clusters of genes *may* (or may not) increase a person's *risk* of developing depression; certainly there is no authoritative claim that genes *cause* depression.

In my experience, depression is not a deficit we inherit. It is not an inherent weakness. As we have seen, given certain experiences we are all susceptible to anxiety and depression. We are all potentially vulnerable; whether we are young or old, mothers, politicians, lawyers, sporting heroes, even psychotherapists. Some professions are more isolating and stressful than others, so it is not surprising to find that a relatively high proportion of doctors, lawyers and returned service personnel suffer depression.

How does post-natal depression fit into this theory? This puzzled me greatly, then a chance encounter got me thinking. Many years ago I gave a talk on P.S.H. therapy at a pain management seminar for staff at Canberra hospital. After the talk I was collecting up my notes, wondering how useful the afternoon had been and mentally re-running some of my answers…

Vaguely I become aware of a middle aged man with a cheery face heading in my direction. Extending his hand, he introduces himself as Peter Jackson, a name I immediately associate with 'Lord of the Rings' movies. He tells me he is a male midwife and knows all too well the link between fear and pain.

"The women I see are often frightened about their pregnancy. They may have had a difficult time giving birth previously and are dreading the prospect of experiencing that pain again. I thought if I could teach them P.S.H. it may help reduce the fear and even lead to them having less pain..." Peter finishes by asking me how he can get training.

"That seems like an ideal situation to use P.S.H." I say. It is a scenario that had not occurred to me. I search my wallet for details of Greg Brice's school for P.S.H. training. Handing over Greg's card, I say, "You will have to travel to Brisbane, I'm afraid; that's the only option at present." Peter appears unfazed and we chat easily for a few minutes before we go our separate ways.

A few years later our paths crossed again. Peter had trained to become a P.S.H. therapist and was using those skills to help women prior to their labour — particularly women who had previously suffered traumatic birthing experiences. Peter went on to develop a program for expectant mothers called 'Calmbirth'[19] that encompasses all the elements of P.S.H. to help relieve much of the fear and pain associated with childbirth. This program has had a transformative effect for thousands of women and their partners and is now being practiced in a growing number of Sydney hospitals — six at the last count and growing. It seems Calmbirth is true to its name and in no small way is helping to reduce the incidence of post-natal depression.

Recently a major piece of research conducted by the University of Eastern Finland showed expectant mothers with prenatally diagnosed fear of childbirth are at a significantly increased risk of developing post-natal depression.[20] This was an enormous piece of research involving over 500,000 women. The results make a clear link between fear (anxiety) and subsequent depression.

However it is not only the fear of childbirth that is implicated in post-natal depression. There is also the curious fact that new parenthood seems to enliven memories of our own childhood, not always happy ones. One client of mine, who had recently become a mum for the first time, talked of her feelings of deep grief and abandonment that had risen since giving birth. She associated this with memories of her father, a rather self-centred and critical man, whom she described as 'absent' — both physically and emotionally. Parenthood can awaken demons that have lain semi-sleeping for years. Just about everywhere we look there is a clear link between anxiety and depression and the sequence is always the same — from anxiety into depression.

There are those who point out that the symptoms of depression are, in many ways, quite different to symptoms of anxiety. This is true. Depressed behaviour reveals a diminished ability to respond — even to the simpler challenges of life; quite different to the hyper-alert 'fight or flight' response that is often characteristic of anxiety. To understand this anomaly, imagine a line showing increasing levels of agitation and worry, a trail of red ink in ever larger font that stretches higher until it tops the page, at which point the 'fuses blow' and the line crashes down below zero. From this point the continuum can be extended down to include levels of increasing severity of depression, from mild and occasional, to prolonged, severe and suicidal. Rather than identify a number of separate pathologies, there is merit in acknowledging the multiple ways the anxiety/depression continuum can affect individuals; a spectrum that begins with mild anxiety, going all the way through to severe depression.

Movement on this continuum is always dynamic. At times we might observe the symptoms as fluctuating back and forth between high anxiety and collapse, then a return to anxiety. A dramatic example of this involved a friend of mine, I'll call him Doug. One day when things were at their worst, Doug was standing in a Sydney train station on the edge of the platform contemplating an end to his suffering. The usual fears of such a violent death were gone. Alone on the edge, apparently calm and in control — but in truth dissociated — Doug felt the train thundering into the station. He knew what he was about to do. Suddenly Doug's heart began racing, his body trembling uncontrollably. He shuffled to the rear of the platform, terrified, and there he remained for some time. The switch had been instantaneous, from dissociation to high alarm. The incident prompted him to get help, but ever since then, Doug has feelings of panic when he goes near that particular station.

In the company of an anxious person, we may well feel a tension, even a sense of anxiety in ourselves. But in the company of someone who is depressed, we are more likely to feel drained. The collapsed state, the slow lethargy, a lack of motivation or desire, can leave us frustrated, empty, exhausted. If I am asked how to tell the difference between anxiety and depression, the answer is found in another question, 'how do I feel in this person's company?' In therapy this phenomenon is known as 'counter-transference' — a non-verbal communication that spans the spectrum of human emotions. In the company of a depressed person my discomfort tells me something about the nature of my client's discomfort — a 'direct knowing' that helps me understand this person's inner world. I make a conscious effort to lift my energy and remain mindful of my changing reactions throughout a session. The rich and subtle feelings felt by both client and therapist effectively form a parallel conversation, filling the communion cup. Counter-transference is increasingly being recognised for its importance in psychotherapy — another sign of the shift in focus from cognition to feelings.

In Australia, P.S.H. therapy is at the vanguard of this shifting therapeutic landscape, but it is by no means alone. Others, including Affect Regulation Therapy, Art Therapy, Music Therapy, Writing Therapy, The Conversational Method, Mindfulness and Somatic Therapy, all have differing approaches but share much in common. They are no longer trying to 'correct' behaviour and cognitive thinking, but instead recognise the client-therapist relationship as fundamental to restoring mental and emotional wellbeing. Within that relationship, these new therapies promote a right-brain to right-brain communication, understanding the right hemisphere's natural propensity to operate at the subconscious level and bring cohesion to the chaos of our raw hurt and grief. These new therapies do not seek to direct and dominate the change process, but rather they encourage our innate self-generating, self-healing and self-regulating nature — more facilitator and less interventionist.

We are beginning to understand the enormous damage

being wrought by severe anxiety to our internal systems with consequences that include systemic collapse and depression. Often we are unaware of our anxiety — as was Darren — but lack of awareness does not make our anxiety any less harmful. Regardless, anxiety can reach unsustainable levels that cause the neural circuitry to blow a fuse. We suffer a nervous breakdown. Depression is a systemic collapse within which we lose our self and life loses its colour. Emotions are the primary factor in anxiety and consequently in depression. Now there is congruence in the latest neuroscience. A solely cognitive approach was always flawed. We need our whole brain to operate cooperatively, left and right; such that logic and feelings come together to get the full picture. Both are necessary to understand depression.

Chapter 5

The Brain That Can't Let Go

With the coming of functional Magnetic Resonance Imaging (fMRI), researchers and medics have been able to see what is happening in the soft tissue inside our bodies. They can, for instance, look at the functioning of the brain without the need for invasive surgery. This has had many helpful applications. Just recently, some clever scientists decided to use fMRI to examine how the brain is functioning in people with depression — and they discovered something extraordinary.

What these researchers found was unusually high levels of electrical connectivity across different areas of the brain, a phenomenon known as 'hyper-connectivity.' Furthermore, this hyper-connectivity remained stuck on high — instead of fluctuating up and down as is normal in brain electrical patterns. Why is this significant? Simply put, these results show how our brain becomes over-burdened and compromised by high levels of anxiety. We have a direct link that takes us from being emotionally hyper-alert to becoming neuronally hyper-connected. One more vital piece in the puzzle of what causes depression. Let me explain.

Recall some of the characteristics of high anxiety — the state experienced just prior to the onset of depression. It is a state of hyper-alert, narrow mental focus and chronic tension. Muscles contract and won't relax, with a consequent constriction of mobility; our neck and shoulders ache; we can't let go. Our whole body is affected, including the organ at the centre of this disturbance — our brain. We may notice short term memory loss, difficulties concentrating and poor decision making. We ruminate, beset with worry, remorse and catastrophisation. Eventually, the brain displays a pattern similar to that taking place in the rest of our body. There is contraction, but no release.

To perform tasks, or direct our thoughts, the brain has to make and then release connections across different regions of the brain. Under intense and prolonged stress, the brain loses its ability to release the connections it has just made. Just like muscles lose their ability to relax, getting tighter and tighter, so the level of neuronal connectivity builds, creating an ever increasing load inside the brain. Each new task demanded of the brain gets harder. This constant hyper-connectivity appears to mark the point where anxiety tips over into depression.

This is precisely the finding of recent research by a team at the University of California, led by Dr Andrew Leuchter. While many of their peers were examining the various functions of individual parts of the brain, Leuchter and his colleagues focused their research on the whole brain and the connectivity across the various areas. What they found was that the brains of depressed people were in a constant state of hyper-connectivity. According to Leuchter, "The brain must be able to first synchronise and then later desynchronise different areas of the brain in order to react, regulate mood, learn and solve problems. The depressed brain maintains its ability to form functional connections, but loses the ability to turn these connections off. This inability to control how brain areas work together may help explain some of the symptoms of depression."[21] Interestingly Darren felt that his brain was always working, always 'on.'

This report led me to a similar finding by researchers at the University of Illinois, Chicago. Lead author, Scott Langenecker, had already discovered from previous research that the emotional and cognitive brain networks were hyper-connected in young adults who had depression. Langenecker wanted to see if there were different patterns in people who suffered several episodes of depression. His research team used fMRI to scan the brains of 77 volunteers while they were resting. Participants who had had at least one depressive episode exhibited increased connectivity between what are known as the 'resting' and 'cognitive' networks, *regardless of whether they were depressed at the time.*[22] This study also showed that the amygdala, a region of the brain involved in the experience of fear, becomes de-coupled in people who have had multiple episodes of depression. When a person has little experience of fear, the usual preventative barriers to suicide are removed. Perhaps this explains why my friend Doug felt no fear when standing on the edge of the railway platform. Fortunately, his shocking realisation came just in time.

Anxiety's pattern of rumination — the constant repeat of

worries and painful memories — places a strain on our brain, which is called upon to first synchronise and then desynchronise different parts with every repeated thought. A loyal servant to the end, our brain makes the necessary connections, but eventually fails to fully release those connections before the next worry hits. Soon a pattern is established where our exhausted brain loses the ability to let go. Still the mind drives the brain into making ever more connections, a situation that can only lead to the collapse of both physical and mental functioning — a situation I likened to blown fuses.

It was a random check on the internet that led me to discover this unheralded insight into the depressed brain. It had received little publicity outside academia, as far as I was aware. However, thanks to my recently acquired understanding of depression as a nervous system breakdown, the significance struck me straight away. I am effectively looking through different eyes and the pieces are falling into place. Here are all the hallmarks of a brain in a stressful response — and I am sure that raw emotion is the only force that could be responsible for such a reaction. After all, emotions create stressful responses in many other parts of our body. We live with tension and contraction on a semi-permanent basis, witness the popularity of massage and yoga — not to mention self-medication — to relieve the discomfort. Rarely do we think of our brain as similarly affected; but of course it is. Now science is able to show us a brain that is able to form functional connections, but loses the ability to turn these connections off. I have no doubt this is a vital part of the depression mystery, hugely important in determining the future of therapy. Not my research, not my work, but nevertheless, it feels like another Archimedes moment in my professional career. What others have termed, 'hyper-connectivity,' I am calling, 'the brain that can't let go.'

Winter is the best season for walking around the hills of Australia's 'bush capital.' The air is clear and the morning sun picks out the peaks and gorges of the distant mountains. In twenty minutes I can leave my home and be on top of Cooleman Ridge, looking east to Telstra Tower across the urban forest of Canberra and west toward the Brindabella mountains. Climbing the hills is good for my heart. Once I reach the trig point I catch my breath and wonder at the view — also good for my heart. The rest of my walk is easier, more like a meditation. It is amazing how my mind, so slow and blocked for ideas when I sit down to write, is brimming with inspiration now in my solitary walk through these vast and beautiful surroundings.

The scent of recent rain — every drop precious — adds sweetness to the grey, wintery green of the fields. Birds, grateful for surviving the stormy night, sing bravely to compete with the wind in my face, loud as thunder. Emboldened by the feeling of vast country, I straighten up and let the wind do its worst. Wide eyed lemurs swing through the scattered fragments of my dreams. Today I have much to muse over.

Foremost in my muddle is a need to match up these findings of hyper-connectivity that seem so peculiarly unfeeling, with Darren's uniquely painful descriptions of depression. His hyper-connected and partially de-coupled brain has struggled to perform new tasks for many years. I may never have a 'direct knowing' of what Darren's depression feels like, but thanks to this research I do have a better cognitive grasp of what it means to be 'moving through treacle,' why performing simple tasks has become such hard work, and why he feels a void at the core of his emotional being. Consequently, I have more empathy for the ways he attempts to survive, for not opening his mail and for the long periods of the day he spends in bed. And that, I conclude, is the value of good science: it increases our understanding of each other.

I recall Darren saying, "My brain feels all gluggy. It isn't an inability to operate entirely, but it is slow and confused; everything takes great effort." This makes perfect sense when viewed in the context of the brain-that-can't-let-go. A brain that finds it increasingly harder to make new connections. At other times Darren would say that his brain felt 'full' and this is perfectly congruent with the idea of a hyper-connected brain. Over many years the connectivity in his brain has backed up to such a level that simple tasks appear mountainous and, try as he might, he can't cope. Indeed, the harder he tries, the worse the build-up of connectivity becomes. Darren felt CBT exacerbated his condition at times, increasing the volume of what needed to be done, giving him more tasks to do, adding more cars to the traffic jam inside his head.

Research is showing us what depression looks like inside the brain. The physical correlates of this deeply mysterious and soul destroying affliction are being represented for the first time. Until now, all we could see were the symptoms, the lethargy, and the despair. Now we can 'see' what underlies the surface appearances; we see how our unprocessed terror, grief, shame, (i.e. our anxiety), ultimately clogs up the brain, adversely affecting its ability to fully function and bringing about the collapse we call depression.

One aspect of these findings is puzzling me. The research shows how hyper-connectivity persists even after the person has stopped feeling depressed. The internal experience of depression may have lifted, but hyper-connectivity is still observable in the brain. If hyper-connectivity is indeed the driver of depression, how do we explain this apparent anomaly? Is this the flaw in the argument?

What strange clarity comes in the morning air! There is no flaw, quite the contrary. I turn to one of the great unanswered questions about depression — why is it that, almost universally, people who 'recover' from depression will relapse again later? Multiple relapses are commonplace. Why? Now, thanks to this research, I think I know. Those participants who were not depressed at the time of the study, but still showed symptoms of hyper-connectivity, may unfortunately suffer a relapse before long. The pattern of hyper-connectivity persists according to a continuing level of anxiety. The greater the anxiety, the greater the hyper-connectivity, until it reaches a critical point where the nervous system collapses and depression returns. We are never truly free of depression until we have defused our anxiety. While ever there is a high level of anxiety, we are subject to an inevitable flare up as life's challenges come around. Sooner or later, hyper-connectivity will spike again and depression will return. These patterns of relief and relapse are common to depression and now we know the reason why. I will need to be alert to these fluctuations occurring in Darren.

Like many, I have long wondered about the effectiveness of Electroconvulsive Therapy (ECT) as a treatment for depression. Why would sending thousands of volts through such a delicate organ as the human brain have a healing effect? ECT had little benefit for Darren, yet there is no doubt that ECT can be effective in certain severe cases of depression. From an outsider's perspective the efficacy appears random. Even the most loyal proponents of ECT are unsure why it works. Hyper-connectivity might just provide the answer, arising as it does in the context of an over loaded electrical circuit. Given the purpose of ECT is to shake up the brain's circuitry, it seems likely that this shock treatment may at times release some excess connectivity. An alternative, though less pleasant explanation is that the voltage is 'frying' the neurones that carry the connectivity. Either way there is relief. But it is a temporary relief and most patients must return at regular intervals for further treatments, because hyper-connectivity will continue to re-build until the underlying anxiety is addressed.

A subtle awareness disturbs my reverie. The path leads me up an incline, coming level to a large boulder on my right. I turn to look at the view, but, grand though it is, something else is calling me. On the other side of the boulder are several curious faces and I realise my progress has been closely followed. There are three at first glance — all divinely beautiful — then there is another. This forth is the cutest of all — diving inside its mothers pouch, wriggling in youthful impatience, and longing for freedom. "Aww, c'mon Mum, let me out." Wise mum is cautious. "Not now, son. Wait 'till two legs has gone." I am the subject of a debate as old as time, the struggle between adventure and safety. Both are essential for survival, but getting the balance right is never easy. Too much adventure can lead to a sticky end, while being overly cautious can keep us in the pouch too long, fearful of life. Keen not to add to the quantum of anxiety in the world, I continue my climb, feeling the eyes following me. I reach the next plateau and have a quick peek back. Mum is still watching me, but her two companions have moved on. Nor can I see her joey from here, so I imagine he's enjoying a taste of freedom.

The next evening I am discussing these ideas with my wife, Deb. There is something I am not getting — what is it that I don't know? I tell her about the research into hyper-connectivity, excited by my discoveries about the causes of depression.

"Well no, I'm not so sure that hyper-connectivity is the cause," Deb replies. "If I understand you correctly, the real cause of depression is our inability to let go. That may seem pedantic, but it's an important distinction."

"But... But..." I stammer. "Hyper-connectivity is clogging up the brain and that's what causes all these symptoms. It fits perfectly!"

"Yes, there is a brain malfunction, but isn't that just a physical symptom?" Deb reasons. "Something must have caused the brain to malfunction. There is a sequence that starts with our inability to let go, that leads to hyper-connectivity, which in turn leads to feeling depressed. That might be important when determining the direction of therapy. Remember what you said about ECT, how it acts to relieve hyper-connectivity in the brain? There is relief, people feel better for a while, but then the symptoms return because their anxiety has not been addressed. But I agree hyper-connectivity is hugely significant to understanding depression." Deb pauses, before adding, "I think your therapy has always been about activating progressive levels of letting go. That's why it works on a more permanent basis."

I'm unsure whether to feel upset or not. I had imagined the real cause of depression to be more complicated than 'just' our inability to let go. That sounds too simple. "Hmmm. Let me think about that." The more I thought about it the more I realised Deb was right. The cause of depression *is* our inability to let go. Indeed, that has been the focus of my therapy all along.

It sounds deceptively simple. Just let go, for goodness' sake! But let go of what? What is it that we find so hard to be done with? In short, it is all the various aspects of anxiety. If we reduce anxiety, we reduce the risk of tipping into depression. If we reduce anxiety, we feel better, more comfortable, more at peace with ourselves. If only it were that easy! Having massages, exercising, eating well, and getting sufficient sleep all help to manage the stress, but still we have difficulty letting go. The physical tension in our neck and shoulders moves up and becomes a splitting headache. Throughout our body, tension constricts the blood supply, ratcheting up our blood pressure. Corresponding thoughts dominate our head — work pressure, financial worries, health issues, or family disputes. At times letting go can seem impossible.

Deeper levels of tension are even harder to let go of. Those emotions that lurk in the shadows, the unconscious affect about which we have little or no awareness, yet we feel their effect. Like Darren's anger, hurt and abandonment around his father's drinking and his mother's depression, stuff he had lived with most of his life. Darren was not conscious of these feelings, only a general discomfort that he could not articulate. To escape the discomfort he worked hard, putting in long hours, gaining acknowledgement and reward. But the rewards were short lived and the long hours exacerbated his problems. Darren was at the effect of unconscious feelings he knew nothing about and was unable to control. Letting go was not possible and the consequences were severe. Depression became a living hell and the physical stress culminated in a major heart attack.

Unconscious emotions are the essential cause of much of our dysfunction and suffering. How can we possibly let go of these? Steven Levine says, 'letting go of our suffering is the hardest work we'll ever do.'[23] How can we possibly let go? Therapy can help, but to be effective it must have soul and sensitivity. Meditation therapy can start the process by helping to quieten the mental babble and let go of our need to be on constant alert. There must be trust if we are to contemplate letting go of our deepest hurts — even though we may not know what those hurts are. A successful therapy will come with skilful means to engage the unconscious affect, our raw and painful emotions — and help us let them go. Restored to wholeness, then and only then, will we realise the full burden of what we had been carrying. We were never conscious of rage, grief or shame before, neither are we aware of their sudden absence. It is the unexpected lightness that we feel — a freedom. Surprisingly, the idea of letting go as a goal of therapy is quite novel.

In the past, psychoanalysis tried to restore our mental wellbeing through dream analysis, word association and talk therapy — in the hope of enabling the therapist to see inside the client's mind and interpret for the client the hidden drivers of their troubles. Freudian analysis was all about making the unconscious conscious. It was reasoned that only in the clear light of conscious awareness, could our pain be processed. Memories of past events were brought to consciousness together with interpretations of how those events led to defensive patterns of behaviour and negative self-perception. Unfortunately, there was little regard for our emotions and therefore there was little chance of letting them go.

More recently we have seen the evolution of psychodynamic psychotherapy and a greater appreciation of the self and the effects of trauma on the self. There is more focus on the healing nature of the therapeutic relationship and less on the therapist's personal interpretations. There is greater respect for our unconscious intelligence and less need to make the unconscious

conscious as a pre-eminent requirement for feeling better. These are important advances in mental health management. Still our taxpayer funded mental health plans continue directing people towards cognitive behaviour therapy. Patience, grasshopper — changes are coming! Slowly we are coming to embrace the idea that mental healing, just like physical healing, is at its core, an unconscious process, best fostered within the shared mind of a caring therapeutic relationship.

In my dreams I imagine telling Freud about P.S.H. therapy. I doubt he would be impressed. By all accounts he was a strong minded individual and, genius though he undoubtedly was, avoided much talk of feelings. He lived in a time before the western world understood meditation and he shunned hypnosis, despite enjoying a dalliance with stage hypnosis in his youth. I find it curious that this man, who brought the world's attention to the power and importance of the unconscious, had so little direct knowledge of, or access to, his own unconscious. By all accounts, he was happy to interpret other people's dreams, but rarely allowed others to interpret his own — not even Jung. Most of his clients were women, many of whom he diagnosed as 'hysterical' (i.e. overly emotional). These days this term is seen, quite rightly, as sexist and disparaging. It was also a way for the therapist to rise above the client's distress and avoid having their own sensitivities disturbed. To be fair, Freud was a creature of his time and had he known of brain scans, fMRI machines and affective neuroscience, he may well have approached his patients, his own self and psychoanalysis differently.

The importance of unconscious affect and the discovery of hyper-connectivity have provided solid underpinning to P.S.H. therapy. Knowing the science has not changed the fundamentals of my work, rather it has endorsed it. Nevertheless, something *has* changed. I feel a subtle shift that is affecting the quality of my interactions with Darren for the better. This is not hubris, although some might think so. I wouldn't even call it confidence. In the past I would remind myself how the very best psychiatrists and psychologists in Canberra had been unable to help Darren. Who the hell did I think I was, pretending that I could do better? *That* is what has changed. Now I believe what I bring to the clinic room will give Darren his best chance of recovery.

At the same time, I am aware that none of this is any guarantee of success. In therapy there are no guarantees. The reality of Darren's condition is complex and deep rooted. The prolonged depression and long years of collapse have had their own traumatic impact. His nervous system may no longer be capable of responding to my approach. That is possible. I don't know. For the moment we must both live with uncertainty. My job is not to be a fixer; my job is to do the best I can to help. Ultimately it will be Darren who gets to heal the painful feelings inside him. I cannot do that for him.

There are some encouraging signs. While in meditation, Darren never feels depressed or anxious. He looks forward to the relief that relaxation brings him. He is willingly drawn beneath the surface, there to be taken on inner journeys that engage his unconscious. I avoid taking him over past events, or raking over old traumas and painful memories. Darren has become familiar and confident with the trance experience, while essentially calling upon his autonomic nervous system to do its stuff. This state of being enables profoundly deep relaxation to occur, and it begins to create an environment conducive to letting go, or de-potentiating, deeper levels of trauma and emotional pain. This is not an intervention so much as it is a co-operation, working with Darren's internal resources to bring integration and healing. These are the same resources, the same corresponding theta brainwave patterns that are engaged during REM sleep.[24] Each of us has the resources to heal, the resources to let go; evolution has not left us deficient. We just need a little help tuning in at times.

From this deeper understanding of depression, we can recognise a few fallacies that still prevail in many circles. Bear with me while I recount a couple, because it is about time we let these go as well…

Depressed people are not relaxed. Darren is not relaxed, he only looks that way because he is not able to do much and he spends a lot of time in bed. He is *collapsed*. This is one of the great misunderstandings about depression — what I call the 'relaxed/collapsed fallacy.' Depression is a collapse, a system overload — the result of a brain-that-can't-let-go. It's still there, all that physical and mental tension. The anxiety remains. Just because it is in a collapsed form does not mean it has gone away. The primary goal in the first stages of therapy is to help Darren relax deeply and quieten his mind, if only for a limited period.

Another fallacy is that depression is a defence, an unconscious or conscious reaction to difficult or painful situations. Depression is not a survival mechanism like fear, for example, that alerts us to the presence of danger. There is no survival advantage to be gained from depression. Sadly, quite the opposite. There is no subconscious plan to it, there are no 'secondary gains.' Darren is not seeking sympathy or attention, in fact he avoids personal interaction. The pressures on his brain and nervous system were overwhelming and something had to give. This is a vital distinction in determining the approach therapy should take.

The idea that depression is a defence or survival response might lead us to question the behaviour as though it were a choice. It might cause us to question 'why?' — the very thing Steven Fry pleads with us not to do. It follows, if this was our choice, then it is a bad choice, a grievous fault — and we must bear full responsibility for it. For Darren and millions like him, depression was never a choice. However, because he could not understand what was happening, Darren felt his condition was his own fault and it was his responsibility to fix himself in the only way he knew — by self-discipline. He would berate himself with terms like lazy, parasite and useless; he saw his condition as of his own making — as if he had a choice. His efforts to try harder, to fix himself, only brought more failure, ramping up the tension and making his condition worse. A damaging outcome from a basic misunderstanding.

Steven Fry's plea not to ask 'why' when confronted with depression was not only because he was tired of repeatedly being asked the same question. It was more that the question itself says how little you understand me and what I'm going through. The search for a logical reason implies there is a logical solution. There isn't, but by crikey, if you engage with this question, you will be told! Be prepared to be 'jollied up'! Unsolicited advice is very rarely helpful; it may even make matters worse. For Darren, hearing those kinds of questions only increased his sense of helplessness and self-loathing.

Emerging from meditation one week Darren tells me:

"I seldom did anything without thinking it through — being very careful. Now there is the realisation, aahh, this is how life's meant to be…"

I hear the 'letting go' response in his words; the sense of lightness, a load lifted. Darren is moving from 'collapsed' to 'relaxed.' He cannot admit it yet, but there is hope. I am further encouraged on another occasion when, after meditation he declares solemnly,

"It feels like I've just been washing all the crap out of my brain."

Everything we do in these initial weeks is designed to avoid adding to the burden in his head. There are no questions about his past, no interpretations, no explanations required of him. He is learning to relax; it is a non-cognitive response, simple and effortless. But it is temporary relief, for we have done little to address Darren's underlying anxiety. Until we do so, there can be no colour in his world, respite will be short lived and he may well return next week feeling 'shocking.'

The move from temporary relief to more permanent wellness involves Darren engaging the unresolved painful feelings that are at the core of his anxiety; unconscious feelings of which he is not aware. The cement mixer that feeds the rock in Darren's chest must be closed down. Darren is ready for the next stage of therapy.

Chapter 6

The Tigers Keep Coming Back

Without a certain degree of stress in our lives we would die of boredom. The build-up of tension and subsequent release is an integral part of daily life, whether it be watching a scary movie, a sexual encounter, or attending a job interview. So what makes too much stress too much? The answer is: when we can no longer return to a state of rest after the provocation has passed — after the tiger has gone. These days, tigers come in many disguises, and while some are just our imagination in overdrive, they are all stressful; they all bring a churn to the pit of our stomach. For so many people these days the tigers keep coming back. The scary movie has become a repeating nightmare and the stress levels keep rising. We can't let go.

My Dad was anxious; increasingly so as he grew older. As a child I never understood why. It wasn't just the deep frown on his face or the intermittent mutterings *'tsk, tsk,'* as he shuffled through the house, or the myriad of things I was forbidden to do because of the hidden dangers that lurked around every corner; it was the very atmosphere in the house that felt so uncomfortable.

"Keys, glasses, wallet," Dad pats his jacket pockets, thuk, thuk,

thuk. "Keys, glasses, wallet," he repeats endlessly moving from room to room. "Where did I put my glasses?" The cushions get a thorough interrogation.

"Peg, have you seen my glasses?" he calls to my mother in the kitchen. The reply is always the same, "Where did you leave them?"

I know what comes next.

"Have you checked your pockets?"

Oh yes, a hundred times…I mutter.

"Try looking in the bedroom," Mum raises her eyes to the ceiling.

Dad swings into action, jogging up the stairs, defying the years.

Moments later he is back. "No sign. I wonder where they can be," he bleats like a motherless lamb.

He goes for the cushions again, looking accusingly underneath. *There's always a chance…* "Nope, not there. Oh, crumbs," he sighs.

These days Dad would probably be classified as suffering 'Generalised Anxiety Disorder.' The scariest time for him was when there was nothing specific to worry about, his fear heightened by not knowing what he should be guarding against. Dad's life was diminished by anxiety. In old age he became convinced he was a bad person, had done terrible things. (Dad was a kind man, who never had so much as a parking ticket in his life.) Conversations became increasingly difficult. His anxiety worsened and he was diagnosed with depression. His last years were not happy ones.

Anxiety is a disorder of our feelings. In that sense it involves our primitive, emotional brain and has no truck with our modern thinking intelligence. Anxiety does not appear logical — but neither is it irrational. It is emotional. There will be no lasting relief from anxiety until attention is directed toward the source of our discomfort — the unconscious affect that infests our lives. But those feelings are so painful, who in their right mind would want to go there? Haven't we spent a lifetime trying to avoid those feelings? Yes we have, but only because we knew no other way.

How can we undertake a journey through the unconscious and fearlessly de-potentiate whatever trauma we find as we go? More particularly, can we do all that and avoid re-traumatising ourselves? How can we ensure we do no harm? The answer is found within the safe haven of *meditative trance* — a state common to both mindfulness and P.S.H therapy. In my work I combine these practices to enable communication to occur at a non-conscious level — in particular with the aspects of mind corresponding to our emotional brain. Unconscious communication may sound paradoxical, even impossible, but that is from a purely logical, left brain perspective. It is of course, a common occurrence. We are unconsciously influenced on a daily basis, just ask any advertising executive! The great advantage of communicating while in meditative trance is that we are temporarily dissociated and will not be consciously affected by emotional memories encountered along the way. Long held wounds can be brought to the attention of our inner physicians, who are used to working while we sleep, processing these pains as only they know how, rendering the feelings benign.

Darren was aware from the start of our work together that this would be different. The switch from therapy as conscious talking, to therapy as unconscious process was scary for him. It took him 12 months from the time he was first referred to me before he could make an appointment. Darren prided himself on his intellect and took comfort from the sense of control that gave him. Letting go into trance took away his familiar sense of control. In addition, because his mindset was dominated by the logical, material world, he was not keen on the concept of meditation, which he initially dismissed as 'tree-hugging bullshit.' Fortunately Darren was able to put aside his fear and judgement long enough to taste the relief of letting go. Indeed, this *was* different and even though his demons returned to torment him once a session was over, still there was some respite and he was glad of it. The next stage of our therapy will determine if these temporary states of relief can become more permanent.

"I wouldn't say I was anxious," Darren's voice has a puzzled tone. He reclines back in his favourite chair as if to make his point, his eyes cast downwards, his head lowered into his shoulders. "I have to acknowledge the depression, but I don't understand the anxiety." His slow ponderous speech and his disparaging self-talk are adaptations that strongly resemble anxiety to me. All of the psychiatrists Darren has seen over the years have classified his condition as 'major depression and anxiety.' Yet he appears confused at the suggestion. True, he does not have a terrified or fearful demeanour, rather, he appears crushed.

I do not try to convince Darren he has anxiety. This therapy does not engage with beliefs, or try to change thoughts. We are dealing with something far more real: feelings. Anxiety comes about because we are unable to process painful feelings. Left raw and unintegrated, these feelings continually re-present themselves, driving our fearful thoughts and muscular contractions. Meditative therapy seeks to find a way to dissolve, or de-potentiate the hurt. To be precise, it seeks to facilitate this happening within the client's mind. For resolving painful memories can only happen within the client's mind. I am not inside Darren's head. I have neither scalpel nor drugs. My only instrument is my voice, and while the voice can be powerful, it works from a distance. In this context, its effect is through resonance and pattern recognition rather than through reason. Storytelling, with its limitless capacity for imagery, analogy and metaphor, is a great facilitator particularly when heard in meditative trance.

I explain where we are going, what to expect and leave the debate about whether or not Darren has anxiety for another time. He is willing to proceed and we begin our first session of P.S.H. therapy. To begin with, this seems like just another meditation. But these are different stories told with emotional intonation, designed to resonate with feelings and unconscious affect. Barely ten minutes have elapsed and Darren is in a dreamy trance, far away from the barrage of negative beliefs and attitudes in his conditioned mind. While the story-telling appears to be a one way conversation, Darren's unconscious response contains subtle clues that require uncommon senses to decipher. His head is leaning ever further to the side, his face has softened, especially around his eyes and jowls and that is a good sign. I am hoping for more. I close my eyes and I, too, become immersed in a state of meditation. Now there is the possibility of a closer communion, of shared mind and right brain to right brain communication.

Among the 'uncommon senses' I experience at this time are variations to my voice, which in addition to being an instrument for delivering communication, effectively acts as a receiver. Most people will have noticed their voice change in response to a strong emotional state. When leading a person into meditation, I sometimes become aware of subtle variations in my voice, somehow deeper, richer, more resonant. My body is constantly responding to variations in openness and connection being felt between the two of us, responses so subtle I would not normally notice. Except at moments like this. Again it is resonance. My vocal organs are affected by these energetic shifts and a heightened sensitivity creates variations in tone and pitch, sufficient to breach my levels of awareness.

The larynx is a wonderful organ, capable of producing finely nuanced communication, so words are only part of what we are saying. In voice guided meditation it becomes an improvisation, where voice portrays feelings and affect beyond mere cognitive reason. I can never be sure how effective the session has been, but in hearing my voice, I get a measure of how connected we are and, by extension, how likely it is that a 'successful' outcome will result. On this occasion, however, my voice lacks that subtle depth and although Darren is undoubtedly very relaxed, I do not feel a strong sense of connection. We have not failed — I am confident some communication has occurred regardless. And maybe it will feel different next time.

Darren is not conscious of the changes taking effect in his mind — just as we are not conscious of the processes that take place during sleep. Morning comes and we are awake again, feeling well rested, our thoughts sharper and clearer than before; we have renewed energy, taking much of the amazing work of our unconscious mind for granted. With this in mind, I bring Darren out of meditation gently, resisting the urge to question him about his experience, save to make sure he is comfortable and clear headed. I need to be patient and will be guided by any feedback he gives me in the next few sessions. My long experience working with anxiety and depression has given me confidence in the effectiveness of this way of communicating. But I have never met anyone quite like Darren.

Over the following weeks I learn more about Darren's anxiety. He reveals a complex interweaving of different emotions; 'shame,' 'worthless' and 'shitful' among the more common. But most prominent of all is a vicious self-hatred. Darren calls this self-hatred 'bile.' "A visceral belief in my laziness and my uselessness — a feeling beyond all reason or logic." I am struck by the intensity of the self-loathing and I am tempted to ask him, 'where does it come from?' Doubtful that he knows the answer, I decide to wait until he is ready to reveal deeper levels of his soul. As it turns out, I don't have long to wait.

For the first time Darren talks to me about his Dad. He adored his Dad and suffered the torment of seeing him get drunk virtually every night. Those evenings when his Dad wasn't at the club he would drink at home. Darren felt solely responsible for his father since his mother was depressed and unwilling to acknowledge any problem, while his siblings, being much older, had all left home.

"Dad's presence had an enormous effect on me, I just longed to be with him," he told me. "That made the times waiting for him to come home all the more excruciating. We knew he would be drinking, but it was left unspoken; there was pretend activity, or just silence. I would feel physically sick."

Darren could never ask his Dad to stop drinking. He could not confront him, telling me later that to have done so would be 'crossing the boundaries of their relationship.' Nor could he be angry with his Dad.

"It was something Dad didn't have the power to control and so asking him to stop would have put him in a very difficult situation — setting him up for more pain. Even as a young boy, my judgements were all surrounded by not hurting him." Instead Darren tried hiding the bottles, distracting his father, he tried everything he could to keep his father sober. His schemes seldom worked, but he never stopped trying.

"There must have been moments when you felt angry with your Dad?" I ask.

His reply is instant. "No. I was never angry with Dad. That would have been totally unfair and unwarranted, because he couldn't help it. There was no element of anger. What I felt was responsibility... failure... loss... frustration at my own inability to fix things." His tone softens suddenly, "It was wanting something desperately — being given glimpses of it and then not being able to keep it. The constant tease of absolute love being ripped away from me every day. It wasn't anger, it was loss — the failure of my childish attempts to stop it happening."

As usual with Darren, the blame is self-directed. I tighten, imagining my own reaction in similar circumstances. His use of the word 'tease' is suggestive of anger. It seems inhuman not to be angry given the provocation over all that time. Nevertheless I believe him. He never *felt* anger. He explains, "He tried his best. I just forgave him."

"OK," I say, intrigued by the thought. "Do you remember the first time you forgave him?"

Darren pauses, taking the question seriously. "I can't remember a time when I *didn't* forgive him. I've always learned to see things from the other person's perspective — making allowances for their weaknesses. That was a big thing with Dad. He showed me reasons why people behaved the way they did. He had this faith in human nature — that's part of the family culture. It is a lovely trait." He pauses, a sense of family pride leaks out. Then he re-gathers himself, "Provided it includes yourself."

"Yes", I say, "you don't seem to have the same compassion for yourself".

"I don't deserve forgiveness." He says bluntly, then after a pause, "And I don't think Dad could forgive himself either."

Next morning the house is cold and I'm enjoying lingering in the shower, the sheer indulgence of these few moments where the only thing on my mind is the massaging warmth of the water. The tired fug from the previous night has gone, and I am a thought free zone. These are the moments when I get the beginnings of a song in my head. Out of nowhere my inner Pavarotti takes flight with volume and gusto that feels wholly satisfying (well, to me anyway — less so our two cats).

But today the cats are resting easy; none of this is happening. A different agenda has been set and it is events from the previous day that leap into my head, eager to be resolved. Darren's words come back, unbidden. *"He tried his best. I just forgave him. I was never angry with Dad. That would have been totally unfair... because he couldn't help it. The constant tease of absolute love being ripped away from me every day. I was never angry with Dad."* Is that possible? Or was his anger shut down even before it was felt? Classic repression.

Wiping steam clouds from the shower glass in a quest for greater clarity, my detective neurones are firing. The daily repetition of intense feelings — whether conscious or not — would have overwhelmed Darren's developing nervous system, causing memories of his Dad to become distorted, or deified, to a point where Darren could not see his father for who he was — a lovely man, but with flaws.

Darren's psychologist had mentioned to me that he appeared angry at times whenever he inferred criticism of his father. In Darren's eyes, his father's image is above reproach. This is not a conscious strategy on Darren's part; in his mind he feels what he feels and his memories of his Dad are real. It's just that they are partial. Darren is not seeing the whole picture. His memories are fractured. My guess is his anger has been ricocheting around inside him ever since the original angry impulse was shut down. But when sufficiently provoked, it bursts out to defend his father and the memories that are sacred and pivotal to his life.

I'm out of the shower now and grab the towel gratefully against the cold. But I'm still turning things over. Darren is so certain in his beliefs and I will not challenge him, nor will I share my thoughts with him; that would be unkind as well as unhelpful. Even my private interpretations feel like a betrayal.

But I can't stop now, there is something else. I imagine his de-coupled anger seeking a cause to rage against. It cannot be his father — it wasn't his father's fault. There is only one person who he can blame. Himself. His father's drinking was a source of great frustration, hurt and fear that became associated in his young mind with his (perceived) failure to protect his father and prevent his drinking — *'my childish attempts to stop it happening.'* From the start of his life, Darren had been inculcated as to the supreme importance of family. This reinforced a strong sense of responsibility for his father's welfare; a set-up for inevitable failure and a lost childhood. The close association between his 'failure' and his immense loss caused the two to become conflated and emerge as self-hate. The bile bubbled up with such intensity that it shocked Darren when he heard himself.

These thoughts, so at odds with Darren's views of his father and himself, are for my use only. They are speculative; I could be wrong. Nonetheless, I do feel better informed as to the nature of Darren's anxiety and I am already thinking of future stories for our meditations. Inspired, I drop the towel and skip down the hall in an unabashed tribute to ancient Greece. The cats scatter.

Darren is looser now, more willing to share his story. He left home at 18 'on a mission.' He got a job and worked hard. He married. He and his wife bought a home and started a family, all in quick succession. A young man, barely 24, his life was very different. He was motivated, gaining rapid promotion. He had left the past behind. What could possibly go wrong?

Darren felt increasingly disturbed, unable to relax with his family. There was little joy in his achievements, always concern to do more, gain the next promotion. Something was driving him to ever demanding lengths. He got a second job, volunteered on weekends, pushing himself to the limit. Whatever Darren did, no matter what he achieved, in his own mind it was never good enough. It would never be enough. As Jon Kabat-Zinn says, 'Wherever you go, there you are.'[25] None of it will fill the hole in his heart. Many of us have childhood hurts that live on into middle age and beyond. Like Darren, many of us are not conscious of this hidden drive. The more he succeeded, the more he needed to achieve — the external rewards bar continually rising. In his own expression of anxiety, he pushed himself to extremes, never finding satisfaction. He was his own torturer, chanting *'I must try harder'* with each stroke of the lash. Pushing too far, he failed an attempt to gain promotion. And then things started to unravel…

Two major structures in his life fell apart. The breakdown of his marriage coincided with a collapse of confidence at work. His wife had post-natal depression and all his efforts to lift her mood failed. In an echo of his relationship with his father, he felt responsible for her happiness, but her depression was unrelenting. Now he had failed as a husband. He started making mistakes at work — a part of his life that had been a source of pride for him. *'But I don't make mistakes.'* Darren was confused. He tried hard to get things right, *'I would take all day to complete a 15 minute job.'* But the mistakes kept coming. His supervisor had little understanding and reacted by taking away all his responsibilities, leaving him with no work, a situation that continued for weeks. Darren was humiliated.

We are rarely aware of the early stages of anxiety. Too late we find ourselves captured and, from then on, our pain and suffering often worsens. Darren's anxiety developed without his awareness, apparently beginning at a time when things were going well — he was building a new life for himself and his family. In reality, of course, the seeds were there from early childhood. The thing is, Darren does not *feel* anxious. He never did. His life was built around avoiding the heartache by working longer and longer hours. It is a common trend — many of us immerse ourselves in busy-ness to avoid those quiet moments when discomfort consumes us. My guess is Darren's workplace effectively stripped him of his major coping mechanism, not just humiliating him, but tipping him over into depression.

Leading neuroscientist, Professor Antonio Damasio explains that emotions occur in two types of circumstances.[26] Firstly, by engagement with external events, experiencing real joys, real threats, in real time. The second type of circumstance occurs 'when we conjure up from memory certain situations and re-present them in the thought processes.' Obvious, once it's pointed out! This conjuring up and re-presenting is an implicit process that enables us to learn from the past, to foster knowledge and to cherish the good times. But there's a downside.

Memories do not form an orderly queue to be re-presented. Like unruly schoolboys, the pushiest get to the front. The loudest, most energised, hold onto top spot, monopolising our short term memory. We all know the feeling of hearing the same dinky tune in our heads playing repeatedly until we want to scream. Eventually tunes go away. Painful memories are more serious, they keep coming back, repeatedly conjuring up the raw emotion that we cannot block out — even after we collapse in exhaustion. We are caught in a replay loop of hurt and loss, prompting a compulsive cycle of ruminating, catastrophizing and remorse.

Fear is the primary emotion we associate with anxiety. But, contrary to common belief, anxiety is not only about fear. Darren is dealing with a complex mix, an emotional cauldron of 'double, double toil and trouble.' If you have difficulty understanding anxiety, you need only think of the witches' song from Macbeth:

> "Eye of newt and toe of frog,
> Wool of bat and tongue of dog,
> Adder's fork and blind-worm's sting,
> Lizard's leg and howlet's wing,
> For a charm of powerful trouble,
> Like a hell-broth boil and bubble..."[27]

Unconsciously, Darren develops strategies to try to limit the repeating hurt. I imagine his unconscious reasoning goes something like this: 'If I work harder and longer than anyone else, if I achieve the markers of external success, surely then I will be worthy of attention, appreciation and self-love.' Apparently not. Finding his schemes do little to relieve the self-hate, Darren's unconscious defence ramps up more of the same. 'I'm not doing enough, gotta try harder.' Even trying a different approach is unlikely to be successful, because the hurt is still there. Wherever you go, there you are. The solution is not another strategy. Resolution will come only when Darren can find a way to diffuse the childhood grief and hurts that live on inside him. Grief and hurt that he cannot recognise, for they are held within his unconscious. He is the only one who has the means and resources to do the defusing, but these resources are also part of his unconscious. Both that which must be acted upon and the very means of acting are hidden from his view.

Anxiety occurs as a result of feelings and emotions that are too strong for us to process at the time they occur. Commonly these feelings are regarded as negative — they create a contraction that feels deeply painful. Some part of us shuts down in response to a state of alarm — a defence, as though in reaction to an assault. Our nervous system is overwhelmed and cannot process the pain. Certain feelings cannot be digested, cannot be diffused in the way most feelings are. So they remain with us, raw, unintegrated, and undigested — constantly reminding us of their presence. They form what Professor Russell Meares calls a 'traumatic memory system' that is separate from our main memory and held in a more primitive part of the brain. Put more crudely, I call this our psychological colostomy bag — prone to frequent leakage. Professor Meares describes the traumatic memory system:

> "Few people can escape small kinds of traumatisation. The experiences of shame and of the fear of abandonment must be almost universal. Where these traumata are sufficient to disorganise and to disrupt the effectiveness of the reflective processes, the traumatic memory will be stored in a different memory system to that related to ordinary consciousness, that is…earlier or more primitive than the episodic system. The traumata are not recorded as incidents, but as a form of 'knowledge' of negative self-characteristics. The individual is as though unconscious of the origins of these attributions,

which convey the feeling that he or she is, for example, bad, stupid, ugly, incompetent, or a failure."[28]

It is as if Meares has met Darren — he knows him so well. Darren certainly does have a 'knowledge of his negative self-characteristics' — they dominate his day-to-day experience and yet he is 'unconscious of the origins of these attributions.' He frequently talks of feeling bad, stupid, incompetent, or a failure — along with self-loathing and more colourful language. He draws from the well of traumatic memory every day and yet he does not see himself as anxious.

To see the complexity of Darren's anxiety is to realise why it is so hard for him to let go. Darren is certainly aware of his self-loathing yes, but in a sense that is not a true feeling. Rather, his self-hate is the 'solution' to an earlier problem. The real problem is his anger surrounding his relationship with his father — the anger that is real, but not permissible. He cannot let go of self-hate because it is not, in that same way, real; it is fabricated.

There is a further complication. Darren cannot acknowledge anger toward his father, because to do so would raise other feelings, like betrayal, or disloyalty. "To show my anger would have devastated him (my father) as a person." He cannot let go of his real anger without causing a far worse tsunami of affect. This is the bind that has kept Darren locked into ever increasing levels of anxiety and finally brought him to the point of collapse into depression.

This inter-woven complexity of emotions can seem impossible for our conscious intelligence to unravel. Indeed it is. Darren tells me he lives behind a façade because he dare not let the world see him. He cannot remember who the real person is anymore. Only Darren's unconscious mind — the emotional intelligence that created this tangle in the first place — will succeed in disengaging from it. Only his unconscious resources can resolve it. Successful therapy must engage at that unconscious level, because that is where the hurt feelings are and that is where resolution lies.

The distinguished American neuroscientist, Professor Joseph LeDoux, maintains that in the throes of emotion, the whole self gets absorbed and there is little or no capacity for self-reflection or self-awareness.[29] When facing the tiger, self-preservation trumps mindfulness every time! The point is, it's not the tiger we are facing anymore — these are slow-motion replays being conjured up and re-presented again and again, but still we are consumed by the feeling of dire emergency. The emotions that are locked into replay mode no longer serve the purpose they were designed for — still we can't let them go. Why not? One reason is precisely because our whole self gets absorbed in the emotion and there is no part of us left to do the letting go. P.S.H. therapy helps us to find that part of ourselves that can do the letting go.

Our baggage is always painful; made more so because of the many ways we are defended against it and distorted by it. But mainly because of its unconscious and primitive location — beyond the modulating influence of our modern prefrontal cortex. It consumes our life to the point where our ability to feel joy and love is diminished, our body is unable to relax, and our immune system is compromised, while conversely, our alarm systems are locked on hyper-alert. It is amazing to think how many people's lives are diminished in this way, yet few realise the origins of their discomfort, even fewer are able to find resolution.

Healing The Mind That Can't Let Go

Chapter 7

My Own Person

"I just want to be myself, not freaking out all the time." Julie has suffered long term abuse. In an act of great courage and with help from friends, she managed to escape from a cult several years ago. She has a new life now and a new relationship, 'a lovely man — I can hardly believe it.' Still she feels terrible, caught in an extreme form of anxiety. I ask Julie if she can remember what it felt like, 'to be herself.' After a long pause, her lost youth wells into tears:

> "No, that's the thing. I was married at 18, after that every part of my life was controlled. It was brutal. I don't think I've ever known what it feels like to be myself."

Perhaps the least understood aspect of anxiety is how it changes us from the inside. Julie's external circumstances have been transformed. She has freedom and a wonderful relationship. She 'should' be feeling so much better now, but she isn't. Her internal world is still traumatised. Julie has come for therapy to discover something she has never known — what it feels like to be free of anxiety. I hear many such stories, although rarely this dark. Most of my clients can remember happier times in their lives and most feel this profound sense of loss; a sense of being changed. Typically I hear people say, "I want my old self back." When we are consumed with anxiety, we lose our selves. But not everyone is aware of their personality changing and not everyone is able to acknowledge their anxiety.

Dad stoops to pick up the newspaper that is lying where he left it two minutes ago — a melancholy heap on the carpet. It's a broadsheet, big enough to hide a dozen sets of eye glasses. He looks beneath, then with another 'tsk, tsk', he lets it drop. He has read every column inch in search of bad news, some terrible threat he must worry about. The paper floats down landing close to the hearth. Beauty, our German shepherd, pads across to tear huge strips off the offending intruder, bringing paper and flames closer together. Dad sees none of this. He is muttering under his breath.

Mum comes into the room, "For heaven's sake, man, you'll set the place on fire!" Beauty beats a strategic retreat, while Mum tidies up the shreds. Dad continues patting his pockets.

"What about the bathroom, have you tried looking there?" Mum asks, going through the same old list. A new surge of hope as he jogs up the stairs.

"Got them." A collective sigh. Even Beauty looks relieved.

But there was a different Dad; times he could be loose and fun loving. Like the occasion of a family day out at Richmond

Park, in London. Mum sets the picnic basket down by the lake, Peter and I spread a blanket on the grass. Beauty heads straight for the water, then emerges dripping wet and proceeds to shake vigorously. Dad shrieks uproariously as he cops the full shower. We all fall about. It's lovely to see his response, because most times he would be horrified and make such a fuss about getting wet. This is my real Dad; the Dad I choose to remember; natural, carefree and sharing a joke at his own expense.

A sensitive soul, Dad had been cruelly ridiculed as a boy by his military, authoritarian father. To understand my Dad and his anxiety you have to know a little about his dad, my grandfather. Hormasji Dadabhai Masani (call me Dada) was a strange brew. Born and raised in Mumbai, he was sent to England to be trained as a doctor. Returning to India he joined the army and rose to Lieutenant Colonel. He served as a surgeon on the Afghan border during 20 years of skirmish and warfare, long before the days of Indian partition. God knows what horrors he witnessed.

Twenty years was long enough. Taking early retirement he returned to England to petition the British government to grant greater autonomy for the Indian people, a measure of self-rule. His family in India was left fatherless, while he made a new life in England.

Even though he couldn't marry my kindly English grandmother, that would be bigamy, she bore him seven children. A mixed race marriage would have been bad enough in those days; this situation was twice damned in the eyes of most locals. Arthur, my dad, was a gentle boy, who took after his mother, a trend that did not meet Dada's approval. Arthur was the only boy and carried all his father's grand ambitions.

The years passed. It was apparent that Arthur was a huge disappointment in his father's eyes. Dada's frustration mounted as his petitions to the British government went unanswered. Not only did he fail utterly in his quest, but his past returned to haunt him. When an adult daughter from India arrived unexpectedly, Dada refused to meet with her and gave instructions she be escorted to the train station. He could not face her, his heart closed with shame. Then tragedy struck his English family when young Georgina, my Dad's little sister, died from septicaemia that Dada, a trained medic, failed to diagnose. Guilt, shame and grief coalesced.

At the sound of the bell, Arthur starts to attention. He has just walked home from playing a game of cricket. Home is a modest terrace in southern England where he lives with his mother and five sisters. His father lives there too, ruling secluded in his downstairs room, demanding each child's attendance by sounding their personal bell. Dada home schools all his children — partly a desire to control their minds and partly fearful of the prejudice that reigns around them.

Arthur smooths down his hair and straightens his shirt, throws a look to his sister Elsie and grimaces. He knocks tentatively.

"Come in." Dada Masani rises to his feet, checks his pocket watch. His frame towers six foot five inches; from this height the extensive white beard just brushes the top of his desk. He talks with an aged, cultured accent.

"How did you go at cricket today, Arthur?"

"I scored 20, Father, and took two catches. They were hitting the ball really hard, but I don't care how fast the ball comes, I'll stop it."

"That's good! I like to hear you being fearless. Now then. I've just finished marking your maths paper," the modest praise strangled at birth. Arthur's stomach tightens. "You'll never get to medical school like this, they only want bright students — not a little fool." He frequently uses this term for his son and has done so for as long as my Dad can remember. Arthur is 16, a touch under six foot and is quick at mental arithmetic. Neither little, nor a fool.

"I'm spending my time on your education so you can follow me into the army and become a doctor. Just look at all these mistakes you've made." He thrusts the maths paper across the desk. "Don't disappoint me again."

My Dad is trapped in a bind; whether to obey his father's wishes, or be true to his own self and suffer the consequences? Arthur clenches his fists. His voice, when it comes, is stronger than he thought he could make it, "I've told you, Father, I don't want to be a doctor — or join the army."

Words and spittle come together. "Really. You think you know better than me? You can't be a mummy's boy all your life, Arthur. Pray then, what *do* you want to be?"

"A school teacher, Father. I want to be a school teacher."

Silence. Arthur's heart is thumping.

"A teacher? What kind of a man does women's work? You little fool, I'm doing this so you can be someone in life." He is beside himself. "Clearly I'm wasting my time. You're no son of mine." More spittle. Dada sits down and turns his back. "You're a total failure. I never want to speak to you again."

Arthur leaves the room, taking the maths paper with him. His bell fell silent after that. They both continued living in the same house, but father and son never talked. It was many years later, as Dada Masani lay on his death bed, that the two men finally spoke. If we are lucky, the finality of death strips away our grievances and we glimpse a deeper truth. There was a coming together, a reconciliation of sorts, as the two men shook hands.

Dad won his struggle to be his own person and became a wonderful teacher. Mum told me with pride that, year after year, Dad's classes got the best grades. In the village where I grew up, students and ex-students alike would greet him in the street with warm smiles and invariably stop to chat. Going shopping with Dad was never quick.

Many years after Dad's death, I happened upon an article in the local newspaper. It was one of a series of interviews with common people in the community. The journalist asks, 'who were your greatest influences?' The old lady replies, 'my grandmother and my school teacher, Mr Masani.' Just one line in a page of newsprint; naturally I kept the paper.

My grandfather's ambitious plans had failed, he had little meaning left in his life and I imagine the traumas of war were never far from his mind. His family was a constant reminder of his shame, but it was the only sphere of control he had left. His many demons were visited upon my Dad. These days it is called intergenerational trauma. The belittling, bullying and shaming of my Dad left a legacy of anxiety; a template of reaction that moulded his future experiences, undermined all his achievements and ensured his condition could only worsen as he grew older.

Anxiety can be passed from father to son, mother to daughter, by modelling and osmosis. I consider myself to have had a fortunate childhood, growing up around green woodlands and free of any major trauma. Nevertheless, I am like my Dad in many ways. I have a similar emotional template. I was a nervous child, speechless in the face of authority, suffering frequent episodes of shame and embarrassment. It seemed to me that I was somehow deviant. I longed to be normal, attempting to model my speech, looks and behaviour by watching the way other boys walked and talked. I had little confidence in my own opinions and therefore never voiced any. My brother talked kindly to me about being my own person. Fat chance.

Echoes of my grandfather have visited me at different times, even though he died before I was born. After leaving school I became an articled clerk in an accounting office in the City of London. My boss was an ex guards officer and I wasn't the only one who found him terrifying. We called him 'Sir' and tried to look busy. After five years I managed to qualify as a chartered accountant and packed my bags for Australia, hoping to find my own person.

Since my thirties, I have sought ways to overcome my demons. The journey that began by learning meditation has, at different times, brought me into contact with many wonderful teachers and therapists. I am forever grateful to them all. Because of them I have become more real, less paralysed. In some respects I view Darren now as through a looking-glass; there are echoes of my own stories, feelings wafting from an earlier life. A shared humanity that does not take away from Darren's story, but enriches it. Still not entirely free of anxiety... Now, where did I put my glasses?

Darren's commitment to therapy never waivers. He has not missed a session. Once again he reclines in his chair — it's always the same chair he chooses — but now his tone changes. "I'm fairly sure Dad was depressed. Drinking was his way of coping. It was really interesting," he uses this phrase whenever he wants to make a point, "it was so unjust, even as a kid I could see (uncle) Neal was favoured — the successful son. Dad received very different treatment." He pauses. "I can recognise many of Dad's characteristics in me."

"Mum was pregnant before they were married. In those days that was a shameful affair," Darren is looking past me. "Dad's Mum was a strict Catholic — a dominating personality." He mumbles something incoherent, I just make out the words 'dragon-lady.' "Mum and Dad were disowned; there was no contact. Neither of Dad's parents attended their wedding. Mum and Dad were struggling financially. My granddad secretly left boxes of groceries on their doorstep so they had enough to eat. I never knew my granddad. I imagine him as compliant, but undeniably generous and good. Much like my Dad." Darren makes little mention of his mother, just that he thought she was also depressed at times.

Darren pauses, always compassionate, ready to excuse others. Even the shaming and abandonment of his own parents — grotesquely undertaken in the name of religion — does not raise his ire. I am silent, not my place to judge such behaviour from a different time in history. Not outwardly, anyway. It does, however, give Darren more reasons to feel kindly towards his father, "I understand why he was the way he was, it wasn't his fault."

The clemency has limits; Darren himself is assigned the hanging judge.

"There was no major trauma in my childhood, no reasons to be anxious. For years I've searched for reasons (for depression). There were none and that makes things worse. It proves I'm a malingerer."

Darren's reasoning is confirmation he is either stupid, lazy or both. This *is* his fault. He alone is to blame for his condition. After all these years his attitude has only become more entrenched, immune to conscious reason and logic.

Progress is slow, but we both sense our sessions are helping. Darren tells me "there's less argy bargy in my head."

Modern neuroscience is providing a new perspective on anxiety. LeDoux describes how the amygdala, deep inside our reptilian brain, plays a pivotal role in our emotional experience.[30] It is the amygdala that first registers potentially threatening stimuli in the environment. In a nano second, incoming information is matched with memory records to determine the level of threat posed. Our amygdala evaluates the nature of the threat and 'decides' when to set off the alarm. Messages are sent along major channels connecting the amygdala to different areas in the brain. Instantly, these parts become aroused, producing chemicals such as acetylcholine, noradrenaline and dopamine that make the cells hyper-sensitive. This launches a full body mobilisation with the prime aim of self-preservation; including all the fight, flight and freeze responses. These are the neuronal and chemical correlates of emotions such as fear, hurt and rage. When the original threat no longer registers, the amygdala stops sending out alarm signals and the body relaxes... except when it doesn't.

Damasio reminds us that emotions are also experienced when we conjure up from memory certain situations and re-present them in the thought processes.[31] The amygdala responds to these memories in the same way as it does to any other threatening stimuli. Whether we have a large collection of painful memories, or just one very painful memory, an endless cycle of re-presenting is quickly established. What began as a passing emotion has become a semi-crystallised condition. This is a model of anxiety as it occurs inside the brain. It is impersonal, seen from the perspective of neuronal and chemical processes. However, it is a helpful guide in the personal journey of therapy.

Remember Julie? She has escaped her tormentors and has a new life with a great partner. She cannot fully live this life, she cannot be herself, because her brain is locked into constant replays of painful memories from years ago. There was a common saying in my youth, 'time heals.' I don't think Julie would agree. Re-presented moments of terror, shame and abuse are keeping her amygdala on hyper-alert, continuing to send out alarm signals, keeping her body and mind in full mobilisation, as though she were still trapped in that dreadful cult. Even the trembling in her body is registered by the amygdala, then treated as a sign of another threat. Anxiety feeds on itself.

LeDoux describes these processes as, 'self-perpetuating, vicious cycles of emotional reactivity.'[32] This is the brain's reaction to emotional trauma. The original threat has passed, but someone forgot to tell the amygdala. To be clear, these are not just random memories being conjured up. They are the raw, painful, fearful feelings held in the traumatic memory; the toxic vapour trail left over from the past. They do not wait their turn with other memories; they demand our attention, jumping to centre stage at every opportunity.

Darren had unconsciously developed a way to deal with his anxiety. He immersed himself in his work. He was intelligent and hardworking, finding relief from his demons in the flood of acknowledgement from his bosses, endorsed by rapid promotion. However, it was only temporary relief — the painful past was never far away. Rumblings deep inside his chest kept returning, driving him to work harder and longer, to get a second job and when that was not enough, to volunteer on the weekend. Darren was creating an impossible burden for himself and his family; all the time unaware of the subconscious forces driving him.

He felt compelled to keep raising the bar; he couldn't get off the train that was heading for disaster.

Human behaviour and attitudes can be a mystery; the link between cause and effect is not always clear. It is a commonly held theory that children who are excessively shamed early in life will subsequently come to think of themselves as bad. My Dad had suffered shaming from his father through much of his childhood and even though he went on to become a much loved school teacher, those wounds never went away. After he retired, my father inexplicably began describing himself as wicked, as having done terrible things. When pressed, he could not point to a single example and yet nothing would change his mind and he continued to confess his 'terrible' past. In his anxiety, Dad's feelings about himself had become distorted and a long way from reality. Shame is a feeling that somehow we are inherently bad — unlike guilt, which is a feeling that we have done something bad. Shame is more personal and much more damaging. I imagine these were the feelings that were re-presenting inside my Dad's head on a daily basis and it must have been intolerable. My father's only relief was confession. They say confession is good for the soul, but that may be more appropriate when the issue is guilt, rather than shame. Then again, people will confess to anything under torture.

Darren does not think he is anxious and is quick to tell me he suffered none of the usual causes associated with anxiety. He does not remember being bullied, abused, humiliated and told he was worthless, ugly, or stupid. He was not trapped in family violence that can be so damaging — love and violence coming as a package, never any safe haven. He says he was not neglected as a child, abandoned, or deprived of love and affection. He did not resort to reckless behaviour in desperate attempts to gain attention or other love substitutes.

Darren appears strangely proud of his reasoning and concludes by a process of elimination, that he must be solely responsible for his condition. His inner critic is merciless, proud and harsh, with one foot on Darren's throat, pointing home the blame for his miserable condition and declaring him undeserving of support or kindness from anyone. No diagnosis needed, it is all down to his laziness and stupidity.

However, we now have a fuller version of the story. Darren grew up in the shadow of an alcoholic father and a sometime depressive mother. There is much to suggest these experiences left a deep impact on his young brain. I imagine Darren felt alone much of the time and at a deep emotional level he *did* feel neglected, unworthy and, if not rejected, then in constant fear of losing love, of being abandoned. Darren is not lying to me; he remembers none of those feelings. Instead he is consumed in the sticky embrace of his inner critic, a cruel antagonist. Not content with daily attacks of self-loathing, the 'vicious little prick' (Darren's description) opposes every attempt he makes at recovery. The smallest improvement in Darren's condition is likely to be snuffed out by reminders of how many times he has failed before and, in a voice of utter contempt, how he simply does not deserve to feel better. Any suggestions of innate goodness or achievement are met with scorn.

Naturally, I don't agree with Darren's expressions of self-hate. On the other hand, attempts to argue with him can sound like a denial of his own experience and cause a hardening of his attitude. Darren tells me past attempts to reason with him all ended in failure; they actually made him feel worse. Of course he understood the logic of what he was being told and how he should feel differently. But the fact that nothing changed simply gave his inner critic more ammunition; 'you really are hopeless, you have the answers and still you're a loser.' I remain neutral and do not engage Darren in reasoned debate.

Each session I guide Darren into meditation, leading him into increasing levels of relaxation or trance, where the rational brain is temporarily sidelined, along with his inner critic. The stories I tell Darren in meditation are 'heart-centred' journeys, crafted with imagery that link with unconscious affect. These stories are told in a way that resonates with the letting go response — the autonomic reaction engineered in us millions of years ago as part of our nightly sleep cycle. Letting go is a necessary precursor to falling asleep, as well as being able to meditate. I tell these stories in the language of dreams, using metaphor and analogy. It will be left to Darren's unconscious to draw whatever conclusions may fit regarding his own life story. For instance, his unconscious intelligence may well come to the realisation that feelings of self-loathing have had their time and no longer serve any purpose. That particular tiger has gone away. That is my hope, but it is not for me to tell Darren this. His unconscious must be able to come to that realisation. Then what follows are the autonomic processes that depotentiate the painful feelings and put a stop to their endless re-presentation. Only his unconscious can reassure the amygdala that the threat — whatever it was — has gone. Engaging at this level with Darren avoids the endless debates with his inner critic.

As yet, I cannot imagine Darren without his anxiety; it is all I can see. Darren does not know what it is to be his own person. Exactly what a successful outcome to our therapy would look like is not clear to either of us. The best I can do is take things session by session.

Healing The Mind That Can't Let Go

Chapter 8

The Four Faces of Anxiety

I can tell Darren's mood the moment I open the door. He appears bowed down, shorter than usual. When he does speak it is one word that sums it up. "Ratshit." He slumps into his chair with no further explanation.

"Ah huh. Has something happened?" I ask.

"Nah, nothing."

"Is your family ok?"

"Yep, the family's fine. It's just me."

Gentle probing fails to make things any clearer. He gets more agitated. Darren is intelligent and articulate — he chooses his words carefully, but when describing how he feels at times like this, it is a struggle to get past 'ratshit.' I know this is an expression of his anxiety. There is no obvious reason for his sudden downturn — nothing in his immediate experience — just old hurts re-presenting. Darren seems to have little understanding of his feelings right now. He is in the grip of an emotional memory, but without any episodic context it does not feel like a memory. He doesn't know why or what — it just feels painful. There is little to be gained in trying to engage in meaningful conversation. I am grateful that he responds well to meditation and that is where we go without delay. My hope is that in a little while he will feel more relaxed, the knots in his stomach and chest will loosen and his head will feel lighter. We can work more productively at that semi-conscious level. If, at the very least, Darren can find a place of peace — in contrast to what he is feeling now — he will take away a new memory.

Memories are central to our consciousness, to our ability to survive and thrive. They are key to our mental health and to a better understanding of anxiety. Without the ability to remember an experience we could not learn anything; we would not even know we existed. When an event is experienced, an unconscious process is set in motion, searching our memories for something similar in order to find meaning and decide how best to respond. Faster than we can think, our magnificent brain conjures up a match, possibly several earlier incidents that feel relevant and we react accordingly.

Most memories are stored in our unconscious mind and brought to conscious awareness by certain triggers. Memories can be evoked through any of our five senses, instantly transporting us to some other time and place. Hearing Billy Joel's 'Innocent Man' takes me back to the time when my daughter was born — a memorable event in anyone's life. It is said that the German romantic composer, Robert Schumann, wrote the piano series 'Scenes from Childhood' after his wife Clara, told him to stop being childish. He was seemingly reminded of his childhood by her admonishment, triggering feelings in him that inspired his beautiful compositions; music that, in turn, evokes memories of young life for millions of music lovers. Memories are integral to our creativity, our wisdom and our sense of self. When our experiences — happy, sad, or painful — are able to be fully processed by the subconscious, the resulting memories are part of a healthy functioning individual.

However, when painful experiences are not able to be processed, the memories form the basis of anxiety. These raw memories, replete with their emotional charge, are loosely grouped in a primitive form of storage — the traumatic memory system — where sooner or later they become *disassembled*. The feeling part of the memory becomes de-coupled from the episodic part of the memory. Once de-coupled, the feeling memory is endlessly represented to our conscious awareness. I refer to these as orphaned feelings because they appear with no reason or context for their existence.

Oh really? That feeling I get of general unease — that's a memory?

A partial memory, yes. Just the emotional content. Uncoupled. We may forget the event itself, but part of its core message remains. Our episodic memory can fail us for various reasons, but raw feelings are never far from our mind. Joseph Le Doux explains:

"...the explicit memory system is notoriously forgetful and inaccurate... (Whereas) conditioned fear responses exhibit little diminution with the passage of time. In fact, they often increase in their potency as time wears on, a phenomenon called 'the incubation of fear."[33]

Memories become de-coupled in different ways. Experiences of early childhood are frequently lost in infantile amnesia, before our hippocampus has fully developed. The hippocampus is the seahorse shaped part in the centre of our brain — vital to the formation of long term memory. Few of us can remember events that occurred before we were four or five years old. However, the emotional brain and in particular the amygdala, is fully functional from birth (even before) recording and encoding our feelings of pain, fear and frustration. When these experiences are not able to be soothed, the raw emotions become autonomically linked with sharp visceral contractions — predominantly in the stomach, heart and throat — forming a sensitive complex that can be triggered (or 'remembered') throughout later life.

Another example of de-coupling occurs in situations of repeated trauma. Research shows that prolonged stress can shrivel the neurons in our hippocampus, ultimately leading to a failure of our hippocampus to perform its routine functions of memory storage and retrieval. LeDoux again:

"In survivors of trauma, like victims of repeated childhood abuse, or Vietnam veterans with post-traumatic stress disorder, the hippocampus is shrunken. These same persons exhibit significant deficits in memory ability, without any loss in IQ or other functions. Stressful life events can alter the human hippocampus and its memory functions."[34]

LeDoux goes on to explain that the hippocampus can recover

if and when the stress factors are removed, although the extent of recovery will depend on the length and severity of the stress. Importantly, the experiences that occurred while the hippocampus was not functional can never be remembered. This has huge significance for therapy. Previously, much importance was placed on consciously recalling the events surrounding trauma, however we now know this may not be possible. Survivors of trauma may never recall the actual events, but they do retain the emotional memory surrounding those events and that is what causes their suffering.

There are other common examples of de-coupled emotions, such as the disturbing eruptions of road rage seen on our streets. These violent reactions, out of all proportion to the often trivial nature of the incidents, point to a hidden store of highly charged emotion waiting for an excuse to explode. Most prevalent and terrifying of all is much closer to home — domestic violence that is ever present, killing and maiming thousands every year, almost exclusively women and children. There are no excuses for this behaviour — absolutely none — but we do need to better understand this most tragic and horrific expression of human behaviour.

Another tragic example of emotional de-coupling became the subject of a number one hit single in the U.K, back in 1979. The Boomtown Rats demanded, *'Tell me why?'* before echoing the dreadful retort, *'I don't like Mondays.'*[35] Bob Geldof wrote this song after a 16 year old girl opened fire on a school in San Diego killing two teachers. When asked why, the girl is said to have replied, 'I don't like Mondays.' She had no reasons for her actions, only a subconscious murderous rage.

The de-coupling phenomenon creates many different expressions of anxiety. This leads to confusion, particularly in mainstream therapy where causality is mistakenly linked with an individual's expression of anxiety. Regardless of the way a person expresses their anxiety, the cause always resides in our emotional memory; not in our external behaviour or cognitive patterns. To better understand and recognise these many expressions, I have identified four distinct *Faces of Anxiety*. It is common for people to experience more than one 'face' at different times.

Full Face Anxiety: Memories arise with all senses fully involved: terrifying flashbacks, with feelings, images, scents and sounds in full concert, endlessly re-living the traumas. This is the most obvious form of post-traumatic stress disorder (PTSD), an extreme form of anxiety, and the one expression where the episodic memories are not de-coupled from the emotional memories. To the best of my knowledge, Darren has never experienced anxiety in this way.

Sketchy Face Anxiety: A vague history of traumatic events is remembered. There is a lack of clarity and detail, even while experiencing strong feelings of fear, shame or anger. It is confusing and we try to reconstruct our memories, filling in the sketchy recall to 'fit' the strong feelings. The imagined scenarios will not always be right, although they may seem a reasonable explanation for the presence of these feelings. In this way sketchy face may sometimes give rise to false memories.

Orphan Face Anxiety: At times we may experience a feeling of general unease or dread, or we may cry a lot and feel inexplicably sad. There are no remembered events that can explain how we are feeling, nothing that will provide a context or reason for the painful affect. The episodic memory of painful events is absent. These disconnected feelings are a common characteristic of our times. This is Darren's face when he comes in describing his mood as ratshit, unable to articulate what he is feeling or why. This is his orphan face.

Invisible Face Anxiety: The fourth face is rarely recognised, yet it is the most common expression of anxiety. It is the anxiety we have when we don't think we have anxiety. Many of us become unconsciously skilled at avoiding painful memories, covering up unaccepted grief with bravado, building a convincing façade to prove we are OK and in control of our selves. We avoid self-examination, because to do so would undoubtedly invoke in us the very feelings from which we are trying to escape. Darren was driven by an escalating need to work harder and longer in his efforts to demonstrate he was a worthy person, and to avoid feeling the shame and loss of his younger self. Unaware of the dynamic that shaped his life, Darren is fooled into believing he is not anxious. This is his invisible face.

I am familiar with all these various faces, having worked with anxious clients for nearly 30 years. Knowing them so well enables me to recognise anxiety without delay, regardless of the form in which it presents itself. Because the cause remains the same, therapy is similar regardless of the form the anxiety takes. Similar but not the same, for therapy must always adapt to the uniqueness of the individual.

Justice Peter McLennan was chair of the Royal Commission into Institutional Child Sexual Abuse in Australia. He spent several years conducting public meetings and listening to the victims of the most horrible crimes perpetrated on defenceless children. Toward the end of his Commission, I was fortunate to hear this deeply compassionate man speak at a conference.[36] He talked about hearing from the victims on an individual basis. People who had never felt able to talk before, who were never heard, never believed. This was an important part of their healing.

What surprised McLennan was the high incidence of victims who had been repeatedly abused over months, even years and *yet had no specific memory of the events*. It was known that terrible events had occurred because of previously obtained confessions. These victims displayed full emotional trauma and had suffered the terrible consequences of post-traumatic stress disorder throughout their lives; tragic examples of the orphan face of anxiety. Until recently, the reason given for this lack of episodic memory was the Freudian idea of repression. We now know better, thanks to our understanding of emotional de-coupling and stress induced changes to the hippocampus.

Anxiety occurs regardless of whether or not we remember the events that caused our trauma. Emotional memories sometimes come as part of a whole memory and sometimes they come alone, naked orphans, stripped of their episodic clothing. Either way, it is the feeling part of our memory that grips us — and it hurts. We feel discomfort, but without a story, we struggle to understand *why* we are feeling this way, or even identify exactly *what* it is we are feeling. All we know is it feels really uncomfortable — 'ratshit.'

Darren experiences a complex of interwoven feelings, but without any remembered events to set them in context, he cannot identify what he feels. His discomfort is made worse by the frustration of not understanding what is happening. Even now, he does not believe he is anxious, although he tells me a story:

"When I was on structured return to work it was the worst time. I felt I was in a goldfish bowl, everyone was looking at me, judging me. Then my boss tells me he has had complaints from others in my section. They say they feel frightened of me because I look so angry all the time. I'm astonished. I didn't realise I looked angry. I don't feel angry." His colleagues were reacting to his involuntary expression of feeling. It is the 'worst time.' Darren feels terrible, yet in the absence of the true context in which these feelings arose, he cannot identify what he is feeling. "It can't be anger, that's not right. What right have I to be angry with these people?"

Anxiety's invisible face often results in an odd type of patterned reaction that sometimes gets mistaken for paranoia. Confronted by orphaned feelings continuously re-presenting themselves — memories that don't feel like memories — we search for reasons; why am I feeling so awful? Current episodes in our life are scanned until, magically, we find a fit.

Like young Josh who suffers aching bouts of jealousy (without knowing he feels jealous).

"Of course, it's bloody obvious, right? My girlfriend is seeing someone else. That look she gave Rowan in the pub last night. I knew it! He pretends to be my best mate, but all the while he's screwing my girlfriend. Of course she denies it, but I'm no fool."

Relationships break up, but the feelings remain. Josh inevitably finds new events, new reasons to explain his hurt feelings.

"John's a piece of work. Did you see him brown-nosing the boss? You know he's taken all my ideas and pretended they're his own! I hate him!"

Josh gets a transfer, another job, and this too, passes after time. Unfortunately, unless Josh gets some help, his orphaned feelings will find new events, new reasons to ratchet up the drama, and so on, indefinitely. Like my Dad searching the newspapers for more bad news to worry over.

A couple of weeks later Darren is telling me about an acquaintance who has twice suggested they get together for coffee.

"Nice bloke, but I'm not into socialising."

"Oh no? But you're comfortable playing the clown during the kids sporting activities," I remind him, recalling his tales of game playing with the local sporting club.

"Yeah, I know. And I often get invited to barbeques and stuff by other parents, but I always make excuses," he says with a grimace. "I don't like having to make small talk."

"Go on," I nod.

"I'm OK when I have a role, like when I'm getting kids involved with sports. That's a façade I've developed, but when there is no role for me to act then it's just me." Darren takes a long pause.

"I don't know how to be me...And I don't know why anyone would want to spend time with me. Just with me." I give him a look, but he insists. "Honestly, that's how I feel." His eyes glisten.

I could argue with him, but I don't. He is opening up; vulnerable. So I hear him, silent for a while just holding his gaze, nodding a quiet 'ah hah', as though any words from me might destroy the moment. I want to communicate through my eyes, something like, 'such enormous sadness...' In some altered space, Darren is remembering feelings for the first time, feelings from childhood. I am affected, I can't help it. This is real. And though it only lasts for seconds, it is precious. Then the shield comes down, Darren's thoughts return and the spell is broken. "That was strange," he says after another long pause. "What happened there?"

The shame and worthlessness that began with childhood neglect is still present in Darren 50 years later. Long forgotten feelings emerge from decades of darkness. The opportunity to feel this enormous sadness creates the possibility of release.

"It felt like you touched something very deep," I answer. And indeed, what Darren was feeling in that instant had touched me deeply. He had caught a glimpse of what was beneath his anger. Something so tender it had cut his soul. His anger, itself covered over for so long, was both a disguise and a defence against these deeper wounds. Layers and layers of cover-up.

Later, in the safe sanctuary of meditation, I encourage Darren to revisit these feelings. There is much to process, much to let go. As always, we begin by experiencing a deeply relaxing place.

In my autumn years, I have come to appreciate a positive side to my own anxiety. The adventures I undertook in an attempt to be my own person form some of my most treasured memories. I can understand much of what my clients are telling me, I feel the parallels, because I have known this from my own experience. People are often confused about their anxiety, they don't understand what is happening and often see themselves as 'irrational' or 'stupid.' I am not just hearing a story about someone else's strange, aberrant behaviour. I have an empathy that resonates with what others are feeling. I see this aspect of my childhood inheritance as a gift to assist my chosen vocation.

Darren has been shut down on many levels for over twenty years. Therapy is slow to take effect; the wheels are a little rusty. It has been several months since Darren first came to my door. Progress is slow; there is a time lag in his subconscious processing that I am having to get used to. Even so, there is less mention of 'ratshit' lately and a few positives are emerging.

"I am feeling a little better," he concedes. "It's like a woven knot that I'm starting to unpick. I've felt a little more spontaneous. For a few hours after therapy I feel lighter in the head. I look forward to these sessions now; it's a break — like a holiday."

Unbeknown to either of us, events are about to overwhelm this tentative beginning. Events that are beyond Darren's control, resurrecting ghosts from his past. And even as this occurs, other feelings will surface. Feelings about which Darren is completely unaware.

Healing The Mind That Can't Let Go

Chapter 9

No Moorings

We are 20 minutes into the session before Darren gets to the point.

"I've been helping Grace to move house. Her relationship is breaking up and she's pretty angry. She's a lot like me — often gets depressed." Darren says, eyes downcast. "She's drinking a lot, gone off the rails. I'm afraid for her."

Darren doesn't usually talk much about his children. His voice is low.

"I want to fix things, but she resents it when I try to help." He says. "I'm sinking back, feeling ratshit, imagining the most terrible news." Darren has been sitting on things for several weeks, trying to contain his own reactions. It is a difficult situation for any parent to witness, though at 22 years old, Grace is no longer a child.

"The last two weeks have been hard, my mind is playing out catastrophic scenarios, full of guilt. If I had been a better father she wouldn't be like this…"

Darren's worry is understandable; there is a real chance this will not end well. The combination of depression, rejection and alcohol is not good. He feels responsible; he must fix it, but he can't.

It fills his head day and night. There are echoes of his childhood that could well trigger a return to depression. I feel for Grace, although I haven't met her. My primary focus is on Darren, but his wellbeing is intricately linked with that of his daughter.

I curse inwardly at this turn of events. Life is unfair. There were signs of a tentative recovery, but these new fears will piggyback on top of all his past grief. I could skip the meditation today, just let him talk. I offer him the option and he says, "You're the boss — do whatever you think." I go with the meditation, hoping it will give Darren a circuit breaker — something to get him past the mental churn.

There are certain rituals that mark the start of each meditation, gathering the mind for what is to follow. Darren reclines his chair with a jolt. The room is warm, but still he pulls the mohair blanket over him. It is a comfort thing. I pull the blinds down, the semi darkness a cue for the relaxation response. We hear the familiar opening bars of music. My voice is strong and engaging, with a deeper tone, reflecting the rhythms of the music. It is distinct from my conversational voice and comes without effort.

The breath is a familiar starting point. I'm going back to the beginning. Except that it's not the beginning. Darren is accustomed by now to these initial stages of trance. Having entered my room racked with days of tension and worry, he lets go more easily than I expected. In less than five minutes the restlessness has left him. His face appears more relaxed, his head is slightly to one side; the rigidity is gone, hands have unfurled. He follows my voice as though caught up in a play, but he is no longer thinking about anything. The mental loops, his worries about Grace, have ceased.

I am not inside Darren's head, but I can tell a lot from his outward expression. The muscle tensions that accompany his worries are visibly beginning to soften. Where is he? You might think he is asleep, but he is not. Neither is he collapsed like before when he would spend most of the day under the blankets. Darren is profoundly relaxed, yet he retains subtle awareness. In the event I say something provocative, even utter his name, or stutter or lose my rhythm, he would be instantly alert. He is in a deep meditation. My aim is to help Darren retain this state for 30 to 40 minutes. This will give his mind some respite and remind him that he can access this peaceful state despite all the torment in his life — past, present and future.

Thirty minutes later Darren is back to normal wakeful awareness. He has little conscious memory of the story, only brief snatches. This is a good response. Lack of conscious memory is congruent with having fewer thoughts and a quieter mind — and a heightened opportunity for communicating with the subconscious.

Darren's immediate future will depend a lot on news of Grace. Wounds cannot heal if continually re-opened. Though he leaves my clinic feeling more relaxed than when he came, it may only be temporary relief. I watch him walk towards his car, feeling a weight in my chest that I am unsure how to interpret.

Three days later, he has heard no word from Grace. Darren feels helpless. "What do I do? I'm sunk right back inside. I'm squirming with uncertainty, no firm ground. Lost, totally out of control. I'm exhausted from all this." Then he adds an absurd, contradictory after-thought, "but surprisingly calm inside."

I pick up. "Perhaps that's the meditation helping?" I say hopefully. Darren doesn't comment. He pulls the blanket up and closes his eyes, indicating his readiness to return to the peace of another trance story.

"I'm getting there," Darren says at our next session. "Grace eventually rang, she came over and stayed 20 minutes. There was no real conversation. I just said I was glad she made contact, glad she was safe. I'm confused, not sure where the line is between telling her how to live her life and not saying anything — just letting her know how I feel." Darren pauses and reflects, "The biggest thing I can do for Grace is to get my life back together."

Three days later he is back, feeling 'ratshit' and 'shocking.' Grace has been drinking and in an attempt to keep her safe, he has been up all night with her. Darren discusses his options and talks about all the things he feels responsible for in the past. He acknowledges that worrying about his daughter is not helpful, but it is all he can think of. "It's all or nothing with me. I can't focus on anything else right now."

In the weeks that follow I never know what to expect. He has a good week. "I've succeeded in putting a protective wall between Grace and myself. Like an emotional barrier. Best for both our sakes. My self-care has improved; I'm eating a bit better. And

I'm having a few wins, proving things to myself, giving myself an identity — an entry back into society."

He has a bad week. The protective wall has collapsed. Grace's problems are getting worse and once again she is his only focus. He enters my room angry and despairing. "Her condition determines my own living. I can't fix it; I just can't do it," he says. "The years and years of things gone wrong — it's too hard. The task is too enormous. Over the years I've spent all my energy and I'm burnt out."

Regardless of whether the weeks are good or bad, Darren's meditations are deep and he invariably leaves a bit lighter than when he came. Several good weeks follow and Darren is feeling more laid back:

"There is less editing, thoughts are just happening, less controlled. I'm getting more confident that things will occur naturally." I wonder if this is the first hint of mindfulness emerging. It has Darren puzzled.

"How did this happen?" he asks. A long pause, then he finds an answer. "When I stopped trying to make myself better. I thought I had to analyse myself in order to get better. Stopping the self-analysis took the pressure off. Reaching a point of acceptance. I was always analysing every thought, every decision. I was addicted, but analysing exacerbated my problems. So for me, cognitive therapy was like serving beer to an alcoholic. Now my analytical side is left to unravel itself. There's less concern for what others think."

Darren tells me with a certain pride, 'analysing is my strong suit.' It had served him well and seen him get rapid promotion at work, but it had become excessive; taken him over and he knew it. It takes courage to surrender your strong suit, but it was not a lack of courage that held Darren back. He did not know how to change. The years of self-criticism demanded he maintain constant scrutiny of his thoughts and behaviour.

The emotional drives underpinning his insecurities have begun to dissipate and as a consequence, his over-thinking is dropping away. Letting go comes from our autonomic self. In the past, trying to let go left him exhausted and more tied up in knots. Letting go can seem so hard. Through the repeated experience of meditation and trance, Darren learnt to let go without trying. With that came a cascade of release.

Weeks later, Darren has an epiphany. "I'm looking at the rock in the centre of my chest. Instead of being cold and hard, it cracks open and inside is a really bright sun. Wow!" Darren is teary for a while. "Really scary. Takes me to the edge." Darren's nature is down to earth, not given to flights of fancy. He strives to be precise in his descriptions. But today he is lost, on a different planet. An experience unlike anything he has known. The rock has been a part of him for years and he knows it intimately. He was sure it contained all the bad stuff. Can he believe what he is seeing? He is silent now, tears line his face.

"That's amazing," I say. "It was the sun inside there." Sometimes it can be a struggle to understand our subconscious imagery. The outer reaches of our memory banks are scanned, hoping for something in our universe that will correspond to our experience.

Anything that will enable our brains to place it in context. There is nothing. His words, 'Really scary. Takes me to the edge,' express his discomfort. In the true meaning of the word it is an awesome experience; beauty and fear in equal measure. His heart hosts a brilliant sun — the gnarled rock split open — all this is challenging Darren's sense of reality. I feel sure the imagery is heralding a breakthrough. This whole encounter might seem fanciful, but it is not his imagination, it is a genuine experience.

Next session the rock is back, as though nothing had happened. I am astonished. Is that it? How could this experience not signal the end of the rock and a shift in condition? Darren's subconscious is showing something momentous happening inside him. Surely that is the point to all this? I try to contain my disappointment. A few weeks later Darren has forgotten the experience entirely. Gob-smacked, I show him the notes and he believes me, but still he does not recall.

Along with other parents, Darren helps to run sports activities for kids after school. It is his one outlet in life. "I'm quite different then. I act the fool at times just to get them involved." I try to imagine Darren acting the fool. It is hard to believe. I ask if he would mind if I come along to watch one time. "Sure, if you want to," he says, delighted by my interest. I get lost on my way to the oval and arrive a little late. It is more than an oval, there are several playing fields, all freshly mown. Walking towards a group of figures on the far side, I am filled by the scent of cut grass, a reminder of my younger days. Thick turf pushes up as I walk. On impulse I jog a few steps, then turn my arm over. It feels good.

All at once I am in the backyard of my childhood, playing cricket with Charley from two houses up the street. Charles is from Australia and a big fan of Richie Benaud. I'm English and worship 'fiery Fred' Trueman. It is serious stuff, we keep a scorecard and enact an improbable Ashes series. Our sparse talent reaches rare heights. We negotiate our way through impossible catches; I have a man over there! It is friendly for the most part and we toss a coin when we can't agree. Entire summers are recalled in the space of a dozen steps, then I am back on the thick turf, smelling cut grass, the nostalgia lifting. A bunch of kids and a couple of adults come into view. I recognise Darren.

The youngest kids are in a huddle; their attention fixated on Darren. From this distance they appear to be doing long jump. Darren draws a line in the sand then crouches down to their level and calls out, "What do we do when someone jumps past this line?" "Elephaaant!" they all shriek. He stretches his head to the ground then lifts it slowly with one arm reaching out from the front of his face, his hand curved forwards to make a convincing looking trunk. A full throated jungle call sounds out across the park and it takes me a moment to realise that this is Darren's voice. The young ones scream with delight, then do their best to become baby elephants. Not exactly Africa; still the happiest of scenes.

Darren leaves the young ones in the care of another parent and walks briskly over to where some older kids are doing their warm ups. He gives them instructions, two laps of the oval, and sends them off with a click of the stop watch. Seeing me, he mouths, 'coffee' and points to his wrist. Fully energised, he is off to another group doing sprints.

When he finally gets a break, he comes over to me smiling and flushed. "Let's get a coffee." He ushers me over to the stall. "Thanks for coming," he says, his eyes sparkling.

"Don't be fooled," he says, sensing my thoughts, "It's an act. I enjoy it, but as soon as I get home tonight I'll collapse again. I expect you're pretty surprised, though, eh?"

I am amazed. Confined to the clinic room, I could never have imagined this side of Darren. Conversely, if this is the only side you ever see of him, you would never know how sick he is. Depression can be deceptive. I reflect on how frequently we hear people express surprise and shock after the suicide of a friend or relative. So often we are unaware of the desperation beneath the façade. The other thought I have as I drive home is that perhaps it is these brief moments in Darren's life that have kept him alive through the worst of his depression. That and his own children, of course. Then I wonder whether, at some point in the distant future when Darren and I are both long gone, those little ones will recollect how they once trumpeted their joy as they drew lines in the sand and smelt the newly mown grass.

Grace has been feeling the need to separate physically from her family. She moves interstate and finds a job and a place to live near the sea. Slowly her life is becoming more settled. Darren tells me the move is good for them both. They phone each other regularly; her down days still affect him, but over time they both appear to be growing stronger.

"For the first time in 25 years I can say I'm not depressed. It feels like the weights have been taken off," he says. "...it's a physical feeling; longer, lighter and looser. Less anxious," he says.

"Lighter I understand, but longer and looser? That's a curious description," I reply.

"Yes I know, but that's really how it feels," says Darren.

"Ah huh." I try to imagine feeling longer, then feeling looser. Definitely positive. Darren adds, "Now I'm searching for something to get my bearings. It feels weird, like I've got no moorings."

"No moorings. That's quite a different sort of feeling." I invite Darren to elaborate.

"Yeah, that's the only way I can describe it, no moorings. Normally I would think everything through to the nth degree. Now I'm responding on impulse and I'm feeling a bit at sea. No solid points of contact. It feels weird."

In the weeks that follow Darren often talks of feeling no moorings. It is an eloquent metaphor; capturing what seems to be a complex and subtle form of feeling. While it appears uncomfortable, it seems to denote a positive shift that is unfamiliar. There is more spontaneity; the heavy hand of control is lifting. He identifies a wider range of feelings, a greater degree of body awareness. I assume this is due to less physical tension and less ruminating. Anxiety represents our attempts to hold on, or get a grip, defending against future physical or psychological blows. It appears Darren's compulsive need to defend himself is diminishing and with that his familiar holding points, or moorings, have gone.

He tells me, "I seem to be dreaming a lot more, not exactly nightmares — but I am agitated, like I'm working at something." A pause, then Darren continues, "My self-talk has changed. Now it's saying, 'it doesn't matter...I might be alright.' Before it was always saying, 'yes, but...' or, 'what if this happens and what if that happens'..." Until now Darren's self-talk was always persecutory, beyond his control. "Being here in the clinic room my words come easily," he says, "there's no effort attached. I'm not editing what I say so much."

"Yeah, I've noticed. That's interesting, isn't it?" I say. Darren's inner critic has had less to say lately. This mellowing is welcome. Things are looking up.

Darren cancels his next session. He has been to his doctor for some check-ups after passing out in the shower. There are blood tests, brain scans, ultra sound — all the modern diagnostic wonders.

"The problem turns out to be a blocked artery," he tells me on the phone. "A 70% obstruction; if it were any greater it would require immediate surgery." The surgery carries risk, so he delays action as long as possible. When Darren returns he tells me about his medical history.

"I had a major heart attack some six years ago. It happened on my 25th wedding anniversary — not that I was still married then. Three weeks later I'm in surgery for a triple bypass. I nearly died, but the truth is it didn't worry me then. If I got sick it didn't matter. Apart from the impact it would have on my kids, I didn't care if I lived or died. In the lead up to my heart attack, my symptoms were unusual. I didn't get any pain as such, no tingling in my left arm, nothing obvious to say I was having a heart attack. Just a hot sweat, nausea, a bit light-headed, breathless, that sort of thing. I managed to ring a friend and she called an ambulance straight away. I remember being rushed to hospital."

Darren is leading to something. "Now that things are better for me, it feels like I've been given a new chance at life. I have a changed attitude that I can only attribute to the therapy. Suddenly I want to live and I'm scared it's going to be taken away from me. I'm terrified of having another heart attack. And because last time my symptoms were not typical, I worry over any little ache or pain and I wonder, 'is this it? Am I going to die?"

"So feeling better makes you more anxious. There's irony for you," I say.

"Yes. In a way it was easier when I just didn't care."

Recovering from depression, especially long term depression, can itself lead to a heightened level of anxiety. Darren's condition brings to light a strange paradox. Depression is brought about by overwhelming anxiety — but in the depths of depression Darren did not feel anxious. His nervous system was collapsed, his energy depleted and his feeling world had shut down. Anxiety had never left him; it was just in a collapsed state. Now that his depression is lifting, there are elements of anxiety re-emerging. It is a diabolical feedback loop, recovery from major depression awakens anxiety. Increasing anxiety brings a return to depression. I am reminded that people with depression frequently relapse after a period of recovery. This may always be a risk for Darren — unless we address his underlying anxiety.

The weeks that follow are dominated by fears of death. Darren is on hyper-alert in case another heart attack is imminent. A sore shoulder, some unexplained back pain fills him with dread. He is ill-equipped to deal with life's more challenging events. He has no resilience in the face of potential threats, firstly to his daughter's wellbeing and now to his own. Once again he can think of nothing else. He knows he is being obsessive, continually scanning his body for signs of impending doom, yet he cannot stop, he cannot let go.

The only exception is when he is here in the clinic room, being led into meditation. Here, for one precious hour or so, he can let go. Not because I have convinced him his heart will be fine, nor because he can see that worrying is a pointless exercise that will only heighten the chances of a return to depression. He understands all that, but understanding will not change how he feels. Darren's cognitive brain is powerless to head off the emotional storms that keep barrelling in on him. He understands the arguments, he has heard them all so many times, but understanding meteorology does not change the weather. Here in the clinic room it is different; we are using another language altogether.

The systems that control our ability to relax are involuntary, a division of the autonomic nervous system, known as the parasympathetic nervous system. This is off limits during periods of stress and threat, when survival depends on staying hyper-alert. In Darren's case, it has been off limits most of his life. Reasoning cannot override this involuntary lockdown; it doesn't work like that. However, Darren does respond to my voice. The familiar resonance of my voice, together with engaging stories and images — this is what affects his autonomic nervous system, opening the locks and offering sanctuary. Each week he experiences deep relaxation and each week is another opportunity to process the stress and threat.

Over time Darren talks less about his fear of dying. Things appear to be getting back on track. Occasionally old themes of self-loathing re-emerge and the self-critic comes back for another go. Face contorted, Darren is berating himself, 'selfish prick,' 'useless piece of shit.' Darren hears the venom but there is something different now. "Hang on. That's not right. That's not fair!" He reacts to the severity of his own words when I read them back to him. The inner voice is the same, but the feelings have changed and the change startles him.

Darren has tried for years to change these internal conversations, telling himself repeatedly, 'I've got to love myself" and when this didn't work he would round on himself, even more convinced that he was a worthless piece of shit. The irony was not lost on him. But with no prompting from me, the barrage is heard and judged to be unfair. He has new ears and a new judge.

Quietly and unseen over more than a year of therapy, many of the painful feelings from Darren's past have been de-potentiated. The power and venom of his inner critic is dissolving. Darren's revelation marks a big moment in our therapy. The self-loathing has stopped its babble. He is fairer and kinder to himself. A major part of his anxiety appears to be diminishing. How this has happened remains a puzzle to Darren. It appears to have come out of nowhere, there were no strategies; he was not trying to be kind to himself.

Meditation is not only relaxing; it also brings about a certain type of dissociation. Whatever worries, hurts or pain you bring with you, they all disappear during the period of trance and for a limited time afterwards. You cannot feel anxious when you are very relaxed. The two states are polar opposites. The dissociation is temporary, but it does create a window of opportunity that is not otherwise available.

As conscious mental activity becomes subdued, brainwave frequencies become slower and our subconscious processes light up. Using allegory, symbolism and metaphor, story and voice reverberate throughout our nervous system and precipitate a chain of innate activity. Autonomic responses are engaged that guide the hurts and traumatic memories through pathways of release and integration. These processes are non-conscious and proceed largely without disturbing the experience of calm. Sounds too good to be true? Well, not when you consider what is happening within you and within me every night while we sleep.

During sleep, our brain weaves a tapestry of memories from

the experiences of the past few days. The weaving process must include a discharge of the feelings and emotions that arose in response to these events. These processes are essential for our sanity; they are the real dream catchers. Shakespeare says it best:

> "Sleep that knits up the ravell'd sleeve of care...balm of hurt minds, great nature's second course."[37]

However, night-time restoration can, like sleep itself, breakdown during times of emotional overwhelm. When sleep disturbance occurs, powerful feeling patterns are left unprocessed and become the seeds of future anxiety. Psychological researchers, Els van der Helm and Matthew Walker conclude:

> "If sleep is disrupted, as commonly occurs in mood disorders, this symbiotic alliance of sleep dependent emotional brain processing may fail. The predicted consequences of this failure appear to support the development and/or maintenance of a number of clinical symptoms expressed in mood disorders..."[38]

P.S.H. therapy effectively intervenes where sleep has been unable to de-potentiate painful feelings. A major function of P.S.H. is to mimic the overnight therapy of sleep. There are two essential stages. The first is establishing a meditative trance, a regenerative state that quietens the conscious mental chatter, bringing peace and stillness. The second stage is the telling of carefully crafted stories that resonate subliminally with targeted emotional and visceral feelings in the mind and body. The effect of meditative trance leaves us largely dissociated from emotional pain and sets the context for stories to encourage the processing and release of these long-held memories. The raw, unprocessed feelings that were creating havoc with our thought patterns, are transformed into a benign legacy. We can relax, freed of ongoing worry; there is space inside our head again.

This shift in feeling states has ongoing consequences. Over the years Darren has collected an entourage of mostly negative attitudes, expectations and beliefs; 'I'm a worthless piece of shit' and 'I don't deserve to be well.' For as long as he can remember these inner voices lobbied on behalf of his unconscious hurts, giving them a voice and reinforcing their existence. Now that Darren's painful feeling states are dissolving, the subsequent collapse of his negative beliefs and attitudes is inevitable. Nonetheless this comes as a surprise to the conscious mind, which is, so far, unaware of these happenings. Now when Darren hears his disparaging self-talk, he is moved to exclaim "That's not right, that's not fair!" A new feeling state is emerging within Darren, free from self-loathing, which will, in time, be matched by new, corresponding expectations, attitudes and beliefs.

Weeks on and there are shifts occurring. Darren tells me, "I am less pedantic, more spontaneous in my responses. I told my sister how I was feeling lighter and reacting differently, less editing, more free-flowing. This movement feels good, I think things are going OK. The spark isn't there, but a bit of unravelling has started."

"Do you still have that feeling of 'no moorings'?" I ask.

"No, not for some time. I can't even remember that feeling anymore. The idea of moorings... it's restrictive, inhibiting. Why anyone would want to live like that I can't imagine. It just feels natural to be free now." Darren takes a long pause. "The difference is enormous."

"Yes. It's like you lived most of your life tied up and constricted. Then, as you began to let go, you are left with a strange, uncomfortable feeling — 'no moorings'. And now you don't notice, it's the new normal." I am excited, but try not to let it show too much.

After another good week, Darren says,

"Just the ability to wake up and lie in bed not having to turn the radio on. That's a big thing for me. It feels really nice, the silence. It sounds simple enough, but I don't underestimate the significance of it. What's happened? How did I achieve this? I don't know."

The phone rings unusually early. "It's Grace here, Darren's daughter."

"Hello Grace. What's up?"

"Dad can't make his appointment today. He's been taken to hospital. He's had a heart attack." I swallow.

"He is conscious though, you can call him if you like."

Chapter 10

Voices in the Head

Darren is on the phone from his hospital bed. His diagnosis has been downgraded. "There's a heightened level of troponin, but they can't find any damage to my heart. They're calling it a 'heart event,' not a heart attack." Rather than sounding relieved, Darren is distinctly irritable. "They're letting me out tomorrow."

"No damage to the heart. That's a relief," I say, trying to sound upbeat. Apparently troponin levels in the blood are measured to detect damage from a heart attack. I assume the levels are only slightly elevated. I ask, "How are you feeling?"

"Dead set angry. This is what you get for feeling better," he says bitterly. "This is the price you pay for all the work. Now that my health really matters to me they're saying, ha, now we'll take it away from you." In the past Darren's venom was directed at himself, now it's 'they' who are the target for these voices in his head. A step in the right direction, I think to myself. His rage is wrapped in a nonsense statement, nevertheless it is no joke. This is a genuine response to feeling threatened.

The anger is still there at our next session. And the next.

Conversation is difficult. I call Don Lawrence, Darren's psychiatrist, and fill him in. He makes a time to see Darren and meanwhile we decide to increase the session frequency to twice weekly. Don is reassuring, saying, "Your work with Darren has been most effective."

There are further tests and the results are relatively good. The degree of blockage in his arteries has remained unchanged from a couple of years ago. It is unheard of for blockages to diminish over time, so this is the best possible outcome. Darren is defiant. "Doesn't explain what happened," he says.

"Yesterday I was real bad. Panicky, nausea, upset stomach. I couldn't eat. Did a lot of dreaming last night. Me talking at my own funeral — negotiating more preparation time…" Through long pauses he continues, "I go through examining my body bit by bit, questioning every little ache and pain. Walking around helps me moderate the catastrophising, whereas sitting still I'm sucked into the abyss. Right now I'm tired, washed out, like I've been through the mill. I yearn to be relaxed and unworried, it's like a longing. I'm feeling lost, confused." Tears fill his eyes.

Darren's inner voice had warned him not to hope, there was no way out, it would always end like this. Nevertheless, he had opened his heart and dreamed his life was becoming lighter. Worse this time, because he had really believed things were different. Amid the gloom, a few good things are emerging; he has stopped smoking and is sleeping a little better. He talks about developing an exercise program.

For weeks Darren is morose. There is little change. It is a testing time for us both. Doubts crowd the path ahead. What I'm doing just doesn't feel enough. I should have more to offer. What would Erickson do?

It is rare to hear the words 'psychiatrist' and 'folk hero' in the same sentence. But Dr Milton Erickson (1901 — 1980) was no ordinary psychiatrist. His unconventional use of hypnosis, his humorous, folksy manner, and his legion of successful case outcomes continue to inspire generations nearly 40 years after his death. Each client was a unique conundrum to Erickson and his approaches were just as varied. To this day, Erickson remains without peer. His genius may have been fostered as a consequence of contracting polio at an early age, leaving him confined to a wheelchair. Sometimes misfortune brings out extraordinary qualities in people. Erickson used the long solitary hours to study people's individuality and the minutiae of their behaviour and communication patterns. He learned to deeply understand people without needing to hear their history.

Skilled at inducing simple trance states, Erickson engaged his patients with stories — he called them teaching tales. His stories had a structure along the lines of a quest; they would build to a climax, followed by a period of relief or success, similar to fairy tales or folk myths. A selection of these tales have been published under the title, *My Voice Will Go With You*.[39] Despite his ill health he maintained good humour throughout his life, to wit his famous quote: "I have no intention of dying, that's the last thing I'll do."[40]

On one occasion, working with a non-responsive patient, he took off his jacket and turned it inside out before putting it on back-to-front. He then invited the patient to do the same with their jacket. This unexpected behaviour, symbolising him joining the patient's 'inside out, back-to-front world,' led to the patient opening up with Erickson, and engaging in a playful banter where change was possible. This was typical of his eccentricity, improvising so as to engage the patient's attention.

Erickson is regarded as the father of modern hypnotherapy. Through his influence, hypnotherapy has moved away from stage show paternalism, toward a more equal partnering that has respect for the dignity of each individual. Hearing his teaching tales with their embedded metaphors, patients were free to apply similar principles and ideas for themselves. They were not being told what to do, or how to feel, there was no pressure to conform. Instead, different parts of the brain were engaged, there were other opportunities on offer, different perspectives on life. Trance was a necessary component because Erickson believed that meaningful change begins at the level of the subconscious mind.

Over the years, I have gathered a wide selection of published and unpublished stories, similar to Erickson's teaching tales. These form a vital part of my therapeutic tool bag, since, in contrast to Erickson, my ability to improvise is somewhat lacking. Using these stories as a framework, I am able to improvise a little to suit the circumstances of each particular client. The type of story that I typically use is a form of fantasy, not too scary, not too saccharin; using imagery, metaphor and heart to engage the senses. A story that while clearly untrue, nevertheless touches something profound.

I look for stories that will meet Darren's current needs; engaging stories that have a strong emotional punch and a surprise factor that will have underlying meaning for him. Dolores Ashcroft-Nowicki has written several books in which she tells wonderful stories, many I find deeply moving. In these stories (she calls them 'pathworkings') the listener becomes the subject of a journey through the mind, into 'a world beyond the world.' One such story, called 'The Night of the Shaman,' tells of a sixteen year old American Indian in the years shortly before European settlement.[41] It is about an initiation rite that is to decide if he will become the new shaman of his tribe. The boy must leave his tribe and his family to walk alone through the night, climbing unaided to the top of a nearby mountain. He is weak and lightheaded from days of fasting, but if he is to become shaman, he must reach the summit and return with a new totem and a vision for his people. He knows he may die, in which event he has been trained to welcome death like a friend. It is a powerful and heart-wrenching story that still brings me to tears when I read it. The quest of the would-be healer. The listener becomes the boy and experiences the journey in first person. I hope it affects Darren as much as it did me.

Stephen Levine tells a different kind of story. From his background of years working with Elizabeth Kubler-Ross caring for dying children, he pours his immense insight and compassion into a series of meditations, many of which verge on the exquisite.[42] With a suitable intervening period of one or two weeks, these meditations complement and balance the questing stories of Ashcroft-Nowicki.

I wind up our conversation leaving plenty of time for meditation. Darren looks weary, sounds weary. In the clinic room he makes no attempt to put on a facade; he tells me this is the only place outside his home where he doesn't feel the need to pretend. Within minutes of closing his eyes Darren is drifting away, head tilting to one side, his jaw dropping. Unsure if there is any part of his mind left to engage with, I raise my volume and pitch, increasing variations in timing and length of pause. His breathing is heavier. Is he asleep this time? I introduce the Shaman story, hoping to attract his attention, but without bringing him out of trance. I check for the smallest sign of response. I can see nothing. The story finishes and on impulse, I add a short postscript:

> "......breathing gently into the heart... a fine, luminous, radiant mist; feel it suffuse the heart with a soft effervescence... Each breath filling the heart, welling over into the body, flooding the body with light. The whole body filled with light... the heart a golden focal point at the centre of your chest. A golden sun... ...and the sun is inviolable... All the weapons in the world could be hurled at the sun and they would melt, they would vaporize.... And the sun in you is inviolable... All the... fear ...all the dread ... the hurt... never good enough...... can all be placed in this sun in you... and they will melt...they

will vaporize. (long pause) ...and in their place — from the centre of the sun — comes an exquisite rose... perfect in shape... colour... scent... texture... deepening and unfurling gently into the light... opening to the splendour within..."

Sometimes there are clear signs that Darren has responded well in a session, but today and for the past few weeks the usual clues are not there and I cannot tell how effective it has been. Darren emerges, somewhat refreshed. That is as good as it gets at the moment. I must be patient.

Our minds are made of stories, from our earliest days to the end of our days, life is filled with story-telling. Stories can be portals into new ways of knowing; some good, some not so good. Darren has his own stories that are telling him life is shitty and he will never recover. His recent health scare is the latest in the series and comes with strong emotional tones, confirming everything he has known about himself. His stories are without climax, without resolution, just endless grief and shame, dominating his system. The power of a story to affect our life is proportional to the level of emotional effect it has on us.

I was lucky. As a young child I would fall asleep listening to stories. Usually Mum, sometimes Dad, would read to me at bedtime and I would embrace improbable characters as intimate friends to be revisited every night. At some point I was introduced to Aesop's Fables. Aesop was apparently a slave in ancient Greece; how interesting that his stories have left a legacy greater than most kings and conquering warlords! Apollonius wrote that the power of his fables lies in how they tell a truth within a story that is clearly not true.[43]

My favourite fable was *The Fox Who Lost his Tail*, about a fox who had indeed lost his tail when caught in a trap.[44] He felt wretched as he watched his friends lovingly preening their long glossy tails. To ease his loss, he tried to persuade his colleagues to chop off their tails and 'be free' like he was. They were not convinced! This story can have many meanings, but I am reminded of how often we grow up feeling that we are not good enough, giving away claim to our true nature, disowning our innate beauty. We are swayed by others who have similarly lost sight of their unique goodness.

As stories grow in complexity they develop layers of meaning. A clever pantomime is designed to be understood on different levels, so children remain blissfully unaware of the double entendre that brings a chuckle to the adults! Many stories written for children have huge appeal for adults. I never cease to be moved by Oscar Wilde's, *The Happy Prince*,[45] and like so many others, I was enthralled by the Harry Potter series.

It is the telling of a story that determines its effect. Variations of tone, pitch, and the liveliness of voice can captivate us. It was Mum's presence by my bed, her rhythm reassuring, her voice entrancing, which gave the stories such impact. I first heard the *Tales of Peter Rabbit*[46] over 65 years ago, but these simple characters remain with me, a memory trail across time. I recall Peter ignoring grave warnings from his mother *('remember what happened to your father!')* and slipping into Mr McGregor's back garden, (that nasty Mr McGregor) and feasting on his vegetables. The story felt so real because of *how* it was being told. I ached to warn Peter to go home; Mr McGregor was coming with a big net on his shoulder and rabbit pie on his mind. The chase was on and Peter was running for his life. Oh, the relief when the terrified rabbit squeezed back under the fence just before the big net came down with a thwack! I loved hearing the same story over and over, reliving the excitement of Peter's narrow escape! Allowed a moment of indulgence, these faint recollections of childhood are present again and there is an inexpressible longing, a sweet sadness for that younger me.

The human voice has amazing qualities. It can make us laugh or cry, it can sound commanding, it can sound inspiring, and it can transport us to different worlds. It was among the first sounds that ever soothed us. Certainly the power of the voice is well recognised in many disciplines. From the warmth and beauty of soprano Dame Kiri Te Kanawa to the soaring speeches of Martin Luther King. Good actors, singers, and orators all draw their power to transform our psychological state from the voice. Therapists have similar recourse.

Voice carries meaning beyond the words being spoken. Fluctuations of timing, pitch and inflection can bring about a relaxation response, inducing a calm, peaceful state (without any directive, or mention of the word 'relax'). Stories heard in a meditative trance can link with our deepest longings, our most tender sensitivities. Many clients uncover a deep sadness that has lain unacknowledged most of their life. The rhythms of voice and story resonate at a deep level, leading to the unconscious release of these orphaned feelings. Emerging from the trance, a person will often wipe away silent tears, without knowing why they wept; just the release of feelings and a sense of lightness.

You might think a soft sleepy monotone would best help an anxious person to relax. Not so. Such an approach can be a subtle form of pressure, up there with telling a depressed person to 'pull their socks up.' A softly spoken, 'calming' voice can often be an irritant to an anxious person, causing them to feel even more anxious. Research has shown that people with a history of panic attacks will register an increased heart rate when listening to relaxation tapes.[47] While this may seem paradoxical, there is an explanation.

Whenever we are anxious, we feel a corresponding need (mainly unconscious) to hold on tight, to be constantly vigilant. Relaxing is felt as being unprepared, unguarded. Implicit in anxiety is the unconscious thought, 'If I let my guard down, something awful will happen — *again*.' When we hear the soothing vocal tone inviting us to relax, it feels like a threat. The alarm is ringing! By trying to sound calming and non-threatening we have produced entirely the opposite effect. Tension and anxiety have increased and we may have added to a misguided view that relaxation approaches don't work. What doesn't work is telling someone to relax. A respectful voice that engages the subconscious in fluctuating rhythms and tone is unlikely to trigger a fearful reaction.

It was over 30 years ago when I first began training as a meditation teacher. In those days I was terrified of public speaking and there was a tightness in my voice that reflected these fears. As a way to overcome my phobia, I spent several years participating in drama action classes and public speaking forums, learning to project my voice and becoming more confident in front of a group. One such course, called *'Being Up Front'* was particularly memorable. We were a group of 14 and every week we performed an individual sketch that was videoed and played back to the class. The aims of this course were twofold: to feel comfortable when presenting 'up front' and to discover and inhabit an 'authentic self.' The second goal was integral to achieving the first.

At times it was excruciating, watching myself attempting to be real, while the rest of the group looked on and gave feedback. Under the kind eye of the course leader Sarah Tansey, my usual affectations and facades were exposed and as these dropped away, so came a subtle change in vocal tone.[48] Four months later, the course culminated in a public performance. One enterprising member of our group, Alexia Miall, hired the drama theatre at the Sydney Opera House. In front of a kind audience of friends and relatives, we each had our moment up front. I did a stand-up act with my good friend St. John (Singe) Miall, during which I was able to incorporate some of the physical tricks I had learned from my drama action training. Midway through our act, I got to stand on Singe's shoulders in a classic upward duck pose, suggestive of an inner desire to fly. At the critical moment, I blew into a whistle that made a surprisingly loud quacking sound. And this is where it nearly went terribly wrong...

Singe is over six foot tall, add my own height and flying begins to lose its appeal. Getting up was relatively easy. Getting down is always the hard part. Perhaps I was too eager. My leap left insufficient clearance and I landed inelegantly on Singe's right foot. It didn't hurt at all and I thought we'd gotten away with it. Until I heard a stifled groan. Don't worry, I thought, the adrenalin will mask the pain. A true professional and a gentleman, Singe carried on without flinching and no one was the wiser!

As a result of these and other courses, my 'meditation voice' began to evolve, distinct from my normal speaking voice; a somewhat deeper, more resonant and fuller tone. Gone the reticence and tightness. This was not a conscious technique on my part; my principal reason for participating in these courses was to overcome my fear of public speaking. I was not trying to make my voice sound different. Nevertheless I became aware of this new voice emerging quietly in the daily arena of teaching meditation. To me it was as though something magical had happened. Indeed, when we escape the constrictions of anxiety the changes often feel like magic.

Colwyn Trevarthen is Professor Emeritus of Child Psychology and Psychobiology at the University of Edinburgh. His work explores how the rhythm of voice shapes infant communication, relationships and learning. On several occasions in recent years, I have been fortunate to hear Professor

Trevarthen talk about his research.[49] He has remarkable videos showing infants interacting with mum or dad and demonstrating their first attempts to communicate. When mum sings a lullaby to her infant, that infant soon learns to 'sing along.' Nothing surprising there, but seen in slow motion the videos show how the infant begins phrases of the lullaby very slightly ahead of mum. The infant is leading the song — suggesting an instant memory of rhythms and verse. This makes music one of our earliest forms of memory and places 'musicality' at the core of our consciousness.

Trevarthen's videos show scenes of typical 'cooing' and vocal responses between mum and infant. When the baby's utterances and gestures are analysed digitally, this proto-conversation with mum is seen as having a rhythmic structure that doesn't just resemble music, it *has* musicality. This new and expanding area of human understanding is known as 'Communicative Musicality.'[50] It appears musicality is a defining aspect of our lives; it is intimately associated with our primary feeling states and earliest attempts to communicate.

I have never regarded myself as musical and cannot hold a tune (as my close friends will attest). Yet, even before I had heard of Professor Trevarthen, I was aware of an implicit musicality in my voice as I led clients in a session. There are rhythms that arise with my words as I relax into the meditation and enter the shared space with my client. They are not contrived or consciously created, but emerge from deep inside me, reflecting the subtle nature of the therapeutic relationship. On special occasions these rhythms and tone of voice feel inspired, as though our shared mind is directing a musical improvisation. Sometimes clients have told me they knew what I was going to say next. They were ahead of me, waiting for me to catch up!

I open the door to Darren. He is on time, a good sign. For many weeks he has arrived late for his sessions, entering with burdened apologies that offer nothing of an excuse beyond a look that says life is lousy. As I see him standing at the top of the steps I know today is different. Something has shifted. He is able to joke again and he is back to calling me 'hocus.'

"I have this desire to engage with life," he announces as I bring in the coffee. "I want the cavalier approach, not this ultra-restricting fear of losing life. I need to trust that things will be OK."

I laugh with relief. All the weeks where nothing changed and perhaps all the time change was incubating. I doubt this shift has come about because of one session, or one story. More likely, it is the cumulative effect of weeks of stories and shared mind space. Perhaps, too, the young Shaman contributed in his own way.

P.S.H. therapy uses voice guided meditation to engage our subconscious mind with stories that can 'feel' like dreams. To be effective, there must be trust and patience and a capacity for what is known in the Japanese tradition of Haiku as 'dreaming room.' In Haiku, the poet surrenders ownership, leaving room for the reader to inhabit the poem. In the words of Carol Purrington, the reader enters the dreaming room with "space... to dream around the bits and pieces and facts that you give them."[51]

Traditional meditation models evolved thousands of years ago to address issues of that time. Amazingly much is still relevant and helpful today. However, evolutionary forces have created a very different modern society. The world we live in has stressors and complex requirements that change rapidly. Humanity struggles to adapt — as witnessed by the growing spike in mental health issues. Voice guided meditation and P.S.H. therapy are refinements designed to help us manage these pressures and even thrive on them.

Darren is back, ready to resume where we left off many weeks ago. More than his words, I can measure his wellness by the sound of his voice. It is stronger now, more vital, reflecting a warmer emotional tone. Where before it was flat and downcast, now it has energy and life. There is a way to go, but he is open to the journey again.

Logical thinking could not have brought about this shift. Cognitive responses do not reach the kind of undigested emotional pain that was affecting Darren. I am glad Darren did not feel the need to cover up, or put on a false show in the clinic room. Glad that he trusted me that much. Glad that I did not need to jolly him up, or talk up the positives. It was not by plans, or schemes, or contrivances that change has come about. It has to do with stories we tell each other; stories about adventure and loss, stories about the quest of a wounded healer, about an inviolable sun and the big heart that transforms fear and loathing into a rose.

Healing The Mind That Can't Let Go

Chapter 11

Feathered Away

Speaking with Michael Parkinson on BBC television, Paul McCartney tells the story of waking up one morning with the words and music to 'Yesterday' in his head; a creation of his subconscious while he slept. His only conscious contribution to composing one of the greatest hits of the last century was to grab a pen and write it all down![52] It is an extraordinary story, pointing to the generative power of the unconscious and the effortless way it appears to operate. Of course, this could only have happened because of the lifetime McCartney has devoted to music. Conscious or unconscious, it's all one mind. It is uniquely his creation, even though he does not seem to know how it was composed.

The characteristics of unconscious creativity are all around us. Like the time Darren saw the rock in his chest split open and inside 'it was like a brilliant sun.' This was a very moving moment for him. What had been implacable and held all the elements of his depression was finally opening up, moving Darren to tears.

The rock did not give up that easily. It returned the next day in the centre of his chest, as hard and immutable as ever. There it remained until one day it was gone, its disappearance passing unnoticed. The rock has not returned. Darren explains it this way:

"I was aware of the rock years before coming here. I had an instinct there was poison in me. I remember describing the rock to Don Lawrence. **One occasion I said to him 'I would give anything to be able to prize it open and deal with the stuff in there.' Now I see it differently."**

Darren **continues,** "The rock wasn't blasted away, it was feathered away. It didn't need a crow bar. It wasn't through impact — but it wasn't that it just disappeared. There was action taken which caused it to go. The gentleness, the non-threateningness, coaxed it out. It wasn't dramatic — nothing earth shattering."

A rock removed by a feather. It is a powerful image, crediting the subconscious with the ability to move mountains. From crow bars to feathers, from conscious application of effort to unconscious effortless mystery. This is a metaphor for Darren's journey out of depression.

Darren describes how he felt about the rock, "The rock contained all the bad stuff, all the hate, the self-loathing, the guilt, my inadequacy. Everything that determined how I was as a person was locked up inside the rock, not allowed out, not allowed to be observed. There was no way any therapy could work with those feelings locked up inside that rock. Not even I knew what was inside there… With the rock gone, the feelings were let out, they were available for therapy."

Another thought occurs to Darren. "The rock wasn't just a security container, it was also a shield against exposure. I needed to present to the world as a socially acceptable person. Inside the rock were all the things I hated about myself. The rock was an assurance that no one else could see the venom. I used to think, if people really knew me, what a fraud I am. That's not such an issue now."

Thanks to Freud everyone knows about the unconscious; we even make jokes about 'Freudian slips.' But when it gets down to the nitty-gritty, most people, Darren included, prefer to put their trust in solid, rational thinking and whatever is physically measurable. Sadly, this underestimates our unconscious mind and ourselves. Our unconscious operates in an egoless, effortless way, often unseen and unacknowledged. It can create timeless love songs in our sleep and heal terrible wounds. Through the autonomic nervous system it maintains life support 24/7. Yet we are reluctant to acknowledge its work. It can build rocks in our heart and feather them away. It is not offended when we later forget these wonders ever happened. When free of emotional saboteurs, unimpeded and congruent with our conscious will, the combination is formidable.

It's not just the rock that has gone away. All Darren's paralysing views of himself, his self-loathing, seem to be evaporating.

"I just find they aren't there anymore — feathered away without my knowing or involvement. In some cases they have been replaced by positive, complimentary thoughts, albeit tentative."

Western culture is largely in denial of our unconscious birthright. We turn a blind eye to the inconvenient truth of placebos and prefer a mechanistic view of ourselves. However, that mindset is increasingly being challenged. Mindfulness is gaining a foothold; a begrudging acceptance in our snapchat, soundbite, fake-news world. There is an avalanche of evidence in its favour. Freud famously declared dreams were the royal road to the unconscious. Obviously he had not tried mindfulness.

Vipassana is a centuries old Buddhist tradition that is becoming increasingly popular across the western world. The practice, known in the west as Mindfulness, is **rapidly achieving mainstream acceptance. Scientific studies show that mindfulness is helpful in a range of ways, including reducing the symptoms of post-traumatic stress disorder, anxiety, and depression. Mindfulness also reduces chronic pain and helps strengthen resilience. It is used in areas of personal development, business management and leadership.** [53] [54] [55] [56] [57] Mindfulness is taught in cancer wards, universities, by midwives, psychologists, doctors and counsellors. Few prescription drugs or medical procedures come close to receiving the amount of positive acclaim that mindfulness is getting.

Put simply, mindfulness is the art of observing or witnessing your various thoughts, sensations and experiences, without attachment or engagement. Mindfulness means paying attention to the feelings of aliveness in the body as they change from moment to moment, being aware of your inner processes, the stream of consciousness in constant flux. Awareness is in the present moment, not captured by thoughts of past events, or fears of future happenings. It is predominantly a right-brain state; a non-evaluative awareness of sensations and thoughts. At the heart of this lies a very important distinction: *awareness is not the same as thinking.* Mindfulness heightens our awareness, while simultaneously quietening our thoughts. When we practice mindfulness there are therapeutic effects that are not easily explained. There are changes that affect our mood, emanating from deeper, non-conscious levels of our being.

Practicing mindfulness does not stop thoughts occurring. If you are human and have a brain then thoughts will arise. A mindful approach is simply to witness our thoughts like flotsam floating by, with a somewhat whimsical attitude expressed as, "it's just another thought..." Over time this leads to a subtle detachment from our thoughts and an equally subtle change in our identity. We are not our thoughts. We become the observer of our own mind. As the observer, we can witness the phenomenon as it arises, but we don't engage.

Our ability to think clearly depends in part on our ability to have periods of not thinking. Without these periods of 'time out' we can be driven crazy by our own thoughts, compulsively engaging with every bit of unhelpful self-criticism, or fear mongering. Darren thought it was his duty to thoroughly engage every thought; not to do so was a lazy cop-out. Now he has become more mindful.

Long term practitioners of meditation talk about 'witness consciousness,' likening our mind to the vast sky and our experiences to tiny clouds. When we become the sky, clouds just float in and out. Awareness keeps our mind open and an open mind can expand, embracing all experience. In contrast, thinking keeps our mind in narrow focus, fixated on clouds, limiting our capacity.

You can be sitting or standing, eyes open or closed, somewhere you won't be disturbed. Five minutes can be enough to stop what you are doing and become quiet. Begin to feel your breathing, the expansion and release, the warmth of the outbreath and the coolness of the in breath. Notice what happens as activity ceases — what rushes in to fill the space? For instance, I'll often start thinking about the things I have to do and maybe notice a subtle tension in my stomach, my impatience to 'get on with things.' I become aware of a desire to move. A mindful response is to open to the discomfort, holding it lightly, while noticing my protestations from a detached perspective.

At other times it can seem to me there is nothing — no inner experience at all; as though in the absence of activity I have become empty. This creates a certain anxiety; I am tempted to search for signs of inner life, for sensations, for something more than merely breathing. The result is still nothing, an endless, empty blackness. A mindful response is to be aware of the nothingness, of my dissatisfaction, of my physical discomfort and hold all that lightly. I remind myself to remain aware of each internal reaction, while noting changes as they occur moment by moment. Like learning a new skill, it takes practice and patience. Unlike other skills, it is not about doing stuff; there is **no goal as such. It is effortless, or as Buddhists might say, it is about non-doing.**

Learning mindfulness progresses in stages; firstly learning not to engage with thoughts, focussing on becoming tuned in to your breath, your internal rhythms, the energetic blocks, then moving out to a growing awareness of your environment. The space you are in will have a subtle feel; being in a small room feels different to being in a large hall, even with your eyes closed. Awareness develops to embrace a multitude of changing subtleties, becoming a most delicate and delicious experience. Gently, don't try; be still and let it come to you, like a wild bird. Over time your awareness will grow more nuanced, without effort. The more awareness grows, the more relaxed and calm you become.

Mindfulness is taught as a solitary practice done in silence. However, people experiencing anxiety find the combination of silence and aloneness profoundly uncomfortable; a space where painful thoughts can overwhelm them. Unfortunately, many people either give up the practice as 'too difficult,' or end up tormenting themselves with 30 minutes of anguish and wonder why they are not feeling the benefits of meditation. My voice guided meditation provides an anchor for people to hold to and remain present in the moment; when painful thoughts arise, my voice is a beacon to draw the meditator back to awareness of the moment. The tone and rhythm of my voice creates an attractive inner environment for the meditator, and carefully crafted stories engage the subconscious mind. Ultimately, as people resolve their emotional baggage, they are able to practice mindfulness alone. One client even manages to meditate while inside a MRI machine!

Recently a friend told me of her shock at the sudden, unexpected death of a close friend. She found herself going over the past, the special moments they had shared. She described aspects of their relationship as an 'exquisite togetherness, the absence of pretence or defence.' Her loss was enormous; in her grief and despair the questions kept tearing at her, 'why?' Many of us who have suffered unexpected loss in our lives will find ourselves churning over similar questions. Of course there are no answers, only more questions — around and around until it feels we will break asunder.

My friend began to stop asking questions and allowed herself to feel this enormous sadness. She told me, "It doesn't matter, the questions don't matter. He is gone for whatever reason; what is real now is how I am feeling. I am learning to live with my grief and my memories. I'm learning to live with gratefulness and loss."

She went on to say that when she stopped the questions and opened to the reality of her experience there was an overnight shift. Of course she was still sad and still she wept on occasion and probably would for weeks, but part of the suffering had lifted. She felt different, released. She asked me if this was mindfulness. I said I thought it was.

In opening herself to the experience of the moment, my friend was able to stop the questioning and the 'if only' scenarios, leaving her mind able to process the shock and loss. The mental questioning had kept her at arm's length from what was really going on inside her. When she dropped into the simple awareness of what was happening — the pain and the loss — then awareness itself allowed the natural process of grieving to proceed. This was not a defence against the pain. On the contrary, here was openness, nothing suppressed.

Mindfulness is more than a meditation technique, it can be a mode of therapy and a way of living. We can practice mindfulness in daily activity — eating, walking, social interaction — all can be done mindfully. Mindfulness is therapeutic when therapy is conducted in a mindful manner. Freud intimated as much when, in the male dominated language of his time, he famously exhorted the therapist,

> "to surrender himself to his own unconscious mental activity, in a state of evenly suspended attention, to avoid as far as possible reflection and the construction of conscious expectations, not to try to fix anything that he hears particularly in his memory and by these means to catch the drift of the patient's unconscious with his own unconscious." [58]

Even in mindfulness however, there are levels of emotional pain at the core of our anxiety that can remain hidden. I am reminded of a client who came to see me a while ago with an unusual story.

Alan sought help for acute anxiety. The main issue was around being parted from his wife, a situation that brought on extreme levels of fear. He became panic stricken at the thought of his wife going away, even for a day or a weekend. Unsurprisingly, this was a cause of tension in their marriage, which he found upsetting and that he wished to resolve. He told me he had suffered anxiety all his life — the result, it seemed, of experiencing a foreign invasion when he was very young. He remembers a soldier entering their home and pointing a gun at his mother, he was aged about three. He believed there had been similar incidents, although much of the detail was lost in infantile amnesia. His mother became traumatised.

They managed to survive and, after the war, came to live in Australia. Alan took to meditation quite early in his life and he had been meditating regularly for 40 years when he came to see me. The meditation had helped him manage his anxiety, however he had been unable to shake his fear of separation. Alan's long established meditation practice meant he responded well to P.S.H. This was fortunate, because we had just four weeks before his wife was leaving for a weekend to visit her family. After our fourth session his wife was about to go away. I asked Alan how he was feeling. He replied that, surprisingly, he was more relaxed about the whole event. In fact, he told me he was quite looking forward to some time on his own!

Through the guidance of P.S.H. Alan was able to reach deeper into his traumatic memory, raising an *unconscious awareness* of the inner terror. With awareness came the possibility of emotional release. P.S.H. goes beyond the normal ambit of mindfulness and becomes a 'search engine' for orphans of our past baggage. Old hurts, grief, shame, terror and worthlessness are brought into a healing awareness, the emotional charge is dissolved and the memory made more benign.

How does being 'in the moment' actually improve our mental health? Is it possible to explain in a materialist, rational way, how mindfulness can bring balance and healing at the emotional, mental and physical levels? The research is there to assure us that it works, but it does seem counter intuitive. After all, we're not *doing* anything, right? In fact, there is hardly any effort at all, so to expect much benefit might seem like wishful thinking.

Practicing mindfulness develops heightened awareness and more right brain participation. There is less conscious effort, less thinking; we stop doing stuff for a short period. Neuroscientists have been taking a closer look at the nature and purpose of the divided brain, unlocking the secrets of the right hemisphere.

The divided brain enables us to interact with the world in two distinctly different ways. The right hemisphere gives us broad attention, the whole picture, inclusive and open to possibility. The left hemisphere gives us narrow attention, seeking certainty by separating out the things we want to attract, or to avoid: the bits to eat, to sell, to buy, or manipulate to suit our purpose. In his book, *The Master and his Emissary*, Dr Iain McGilchrist explains how the evolutionary advantage of the split brain can be seen in the behaviour of a bird (birds also have a split brain) who must frequently perform two very different tasks. She must focus attention narrowly on a seed of grain to eat, while at the same time maintain a constant awareness of the surrounding environment to guard against predators. Both tasks are complex and vital to survival.[59]

McGilchrist points out that the two hemispheres are asymmetrical (not mirror images of each other). He explains they have different ways of operating, reflecting different ways of being in the world. They present opposing world views, each operates to inhibit the other, yet their relationship is symbiotic, as both are essential to our healthy functioning.

Our present day bias toward the more impersonal style of the left hemisphere reflects a malaise that is seen, amongst other things, in social fragmentation, loneliness, and the mental health crises engulfing much of western civilisation. The role of the right hemisphere is vital for healing our world. The right brain values relationship and creativity, which are often dismissed as unproductive, belittled by a culture that disproportionately seeks measurement, testing, control and certainty — all left brain styles of operating. Without mentioning mindfulness, McGilchrist makes clear how and why such a practice is so beneficial. Drawing from vast volumes of evidence, including brain scans from people who have suffered damage to one side of their brain or the other, McGilchrist describes the brain's right hemisphere as having a wide focus: everything is connected, in context and irreducible. Because it sees connections it can understand humour and metaphor; it can identify emotional expression, vocal intonation and gesture. It can also embrace ambiguity and paradox; it sees things in their context and thus cannot think in abstract. Whereas the left brain focuses on one part of the whole picture in order to mould or control that part to its own advantage. It seeks certainty; its concern is with the objective, the impersonal. It has a narrow focus.

Similarly, Professor Russell Meares states:

"...the left hemisphere (is) analytic, focussed on the details, whereas the right hemisphere has a synthetic function enabling us to create coherence out of the mass of sensory data impinging upon us at any moment."[60]

It is apparent that mindfulness is predominantly a right brain practice. A mindful approach witnesses what is experienced; it does not engage in thinking about the experience, it is the experience. It is equally apparent that anxious behaviour in its various forms is predominantly left brain in nature. A common feature of anxiety is over-thinking, a narrow focus that engages with particular thoughts. When Darren was caught up in anxiety about his daughter he told me, "It's all or nothing with me. I can't turn my attention to anything else. It's exhausting." His response was the same when he was consumed with worry about his own health.

A regular mindfulness practice will bring more right brain influence to bear. It lifts us out of patterns of analysis-paralysis into a bigger world view that can create coherence out of chaos. All of which sounds like healing to me. Unsurprisingly, McGilchrist points out that healing, relaxation and, indeed unconscious thought are all right brain dominant processes.

Jodie enters my clinic room in tears. It is her first visit. She sits down and grabs at the box of tissues. I offer her a cup of tea (the oldest therapy in the book) but she shakes her head. She tries vainly to cover her raw emotions and her panda-face, disappearing behind handfuls of tissues. I discretely place a waste paper basket close to her chair and wait patiently to hear her story.

Jodie's partner of five years has expressed a wish to end their relationship. Jodie's pain is acute, made worse by her partner's vacillation and hedging, leaving open the possibility for a change of heart. Though I'm sure it was not deliberately cruel, the term 'cat and mouse' comes to mind. Rasping sobs punctuate descriptions of imagined reconciliation and ways she might bring that about. I am unsure how to help her. I don't think talking her through these abstract possibilities is going to help at this point, nor can I imagine her settling into meditation. I need to act quickly.

Through her tears I ask her to find the place in her body that is hurting the most. Jodie indicates her heart and then her tummy. I ask her to focus on her tummy, to describe the discomfort and to place her hand over the affected area.

"Close your eyes and imagine breathing into the discomfort. Explore the sensation, even though it hurts. As much as you can, open yourself to the physical expression of pain. Find the edges where pain ends. Colour it in between the lines, this painful shape. Dull grey, perhaps, or mission brown." Jodie follows my instructions while the weeping continues. "Keep your awareness on the discomfort, notice if there are any changes occurring. Now breathe a little slower...a little deeper." I give her a minute of silence, watching the jerky breath becoming a little more even.

"Imagine breathing into the pain, breathing in white light... breathing out the grey, the dirty brown..." Another moment of silence. "Keep focussing on the area of discomfort — notice if it changes at all; if it moves about, becomes bigger or smaller." A longer silence. I realise the weeping has stopped. In less than five minutes Jodie opens her eyes and declares the pain has gone. She speaks quietly and slowly. "I do feel better ... my head is quieter and calmer."

This is mindfulness in action. There was no attempt to find a solution to Jodie's predicament. I did not engage her in thinking through schemes and scenarios. Yet her emotional state improved. The reason? Jodie switched from frenetic, narrow focus, left brain dominant patterns of thinking that locked in her feelings of distress, to openly receiving what she was feeling. She was able to maintain awareness of the physical sensations in her stomach even though they were uncomfortable. This awareness became her state of mind, replacing the barrage of thinking, planning and catastrophising that had been filling her head. Practicing body awareness helped her to stop the endless thinking, 'to get out of her head.' To her enormous credit she remained open in that way, noting how the feelings changed moment to moment. Through her awareness came right brain coherence, agitation ceased, calmness settled.

Darren sums up his feelings. The prisons of his past are being feathered away, revealing a growing sense of mindfulness:

"I do feel fairly peaceful and serene, well beyond what I would have hoped for. This is not a feeling contingent upon achievement or situation. It's not a state reliant on externalities. I wouldn't use the word 'happiness.' The good thing is I can be sad within this place. It transcends happiness and sadness. This is a state where happiness and sadness can co-exist. No labels, it is nothing I've pursued, just where I've landed at the moment. The important thing has been the consistency, the regularity. Short term satisfaction was never on my radar."

Mindfulness is not a reference to mind as a container with no spare capacity. It refers to a mind that has access to a vast array of resources and abilities. Mindfulness is a means of restoring trust in ourselves, arriving fresh to the experience of each new moment. We are not stuck on an event or point in the continuum of time. The mindless pursuit of future happiness gives way to a genuine appreciation of the present. By emphasising the role of the right hemisphere, both halves of the brain can function more effectively.

The possibilities of mindfulness go beyond those aspects of ourselves normally considered conscious. With P.S.H. therapy and voice guided meditation, Darren has been able to expand mindfulness into the shunned and shadowy parts of his unconscious. Silently, without knowing how he got here, he has awoken to the music of his own love song. '...peaceful and serene...not a feeling contingent upon achievement or situation... It transcends happiness and sadness... well beyond what I would have hoped for.'

Chapter 12

Don't Ask Me to Change

Sometimes the most innocent sounding question can set off a surprising response. Darren settles in his chair with a plate of toast with honey. I hand him his coffee, white and two.

"Any change this week?" I ask, immediately regretting my choice of words.

"Don't ask me to change," he says.

His mood is in contrast to how he was when he left last week. He is not distressed, but the recent highs are gone. He eats his toast reluctantly. A lasting effect of his depression has been a loss of appetite and little enjoyment of food. Coffee is his chief addiction.

A surge of irritation wells up in me. This is not the first time Darren has objected to the word 'change.' How can he want to get better and not want to change? Why wouldn't he want to change? He is changing! I say none of this, but silently continue my rant. There are clear signs you are feeling better, a change for the good. What are you really trying to tell me?

As we chat, I recount some of the changes in him:

"You don't get depressed, and life feels lighter, you're not shovelling through treacle and fog any more. You've come so far, your self-talk is kinder and you even speak of liking yourself. All positive changes."

The effect is not what I hoped for. The more I try to convince him, the stronger his resolve. He tells me that it may only be temporary. Wellness is foreign and the fear of regressing has returned. He can't risk getting too attached to feeling well. I hope he doesn't give up now. That would be a travesty.

"Many times I've felt hope," he says "only for it to be snuffed out. I'm left thinking, how stupid was I? There were so many failures and each time it hurt more." Just the thought of change is a trigger for his anxiety.

There is something else going on. I ask, "So, tell me more about change. What does that mean to you?"

"Change is a word I hate. It implies responsibility, being wrong or bad; it makes things almost impossible. It's really important that I'm not bad," he says.

"Can you suggest a better word?" I ask.

"Choice is a nice word," he replies. "It's important for me to know I'm going towards something rather than away from something. I want to find out about me — not throwing anything away. I'm moving toward being able to think in the absence of fear — fear of judgement, being wrong, inappropriate, or not meeting expectations."

"Choice implies competence and confidence, a degree of self-belief," I say.

"In my gut, I feel like I'm moving toward choice, not moving to change," he says. "Things unfold. I like to use the word 'unfold,' suggesting it's not up to me. It's like reading the next chapter of a new book, to see where it takes me. The responsibility is not mine."

I am beginning to understand. "It's a relief not to feel responsible all the time," I say.

"When I was at my worst, I felt responsible for everyone," Darren says. "My father, my marriage; I couldn't fix them. My work. Everything in my life was set in concrete. A lot of my lethargy was caused by feeling it was all up to me. The burden of responsibility was too great. So the alternative, 'funny how things unfold,' can lift the burden a little."

All those years Darren was trying to fix his father's drinking, then his wife's depression, but he never could. It was not for lack of trying. His words are telling, 'The burden of responsibility was too great.' An unbearable burden, because from his earliest days, his efforts to change his father's drinking were all a failure. He was a failure. The very idea of change maybe a link back to his past.

"Before it was a different starting-off point, feeling hopeless, not good at anything. I was grasping at opportunities to prove I was worthwhile. But no amount of proof was ever enough..." As he talks, Darren recalls an incident that happened shortly before he started seeing me:

"I was doing a CIT class in sports coaching. The lecturer takes me aside and says, 'Darren, you've topped the class!' I was unable to accept the praise, unable to accept that I had produced quality. I replied, 'doesn't say much for the rest of them, does it?'"

How curious. Here was proof that he was doing something well and instead of being welcomed, it is batted away in contempt. The lecturer's news did not fit with his view of himself and he would hear none of it. Darren withdrew from the course shortly afterwards, unable to give a rational explanation.

"Back then I used every word to insult myself — with real venom," he says. "I held these fundamental attitudes and beliefs about myself that I would defend to the death."

Now some of the emotionally charged baggage has dissolved. He is less defensive, ready to move on. In his peculiarly pedantic way, he acknowledges there are differences now, but not changes.

"...this (therapy) is quite different from anything else I've ever done. It's not about me, I don't have to change me. I'm more aware of things. I am free to sit back and observe. This is what makes it real. How did it happen? I don't know."

Darren continues, "Partly it was the environment. It was feeling safe: there was no checking to see if what I was saying was acceptable. Instead of feeling a need for me to change, I had freedom to observe. That was critical, because needing to change would immediately involve the inner critic. I can hear his voice, 'C'mon, try harder! Don't be lazy, be sure this makes sense, think it through...' Whenever change is mentioned I'm hooked back into the poison."

A few weeks later Darren returns to the theme:

"I feel a growing trust in this process and increasing calmness." Looking at me he repeats, "...but how it happened I don't know...I was always cautious around voicing positives. There were real dangers in setting myself up for disappointment. The guarded approach kept me alive — but also kept me more entrenched. So I didn't learn optimism from my head. My subconscious became optimistic before I became aware of it. I have optimism now — it comes from how I feel, not how I think..." After a period of silence he goes on:

"Calmness comes from the meditation. Trust grows from not having solutions presented to me. You're listening to me; patient, not 'treating' me, nonthreatening. I'm not required to change. I seldom find myself answering questions, I'm just talking. Not the classic 'open questions,' just open to self-reflection."

Darren is describing the essence of unfolding, self-transformation; identifying differences without knowing how they have come about. In some ways this is the antithesis of positive psychology or cognitive therapy. He is not pretending to be happy; it is not some version of 'fake it 'till you make it.' There is no 'analysing.' The feelings he describes are emerging naturally from within him.

A week later Darren expands further:

"This therapy is letting loose an inner goodness; I'm thinking 'I'm ok, there are good aspects.' Over time there has come an acceptance and regard for myself. Nothing has changed. I'm still working with the same material, but I'm viewing it in a different light."

Darren continues, "If I'm asked, 'what did I do to get out of depression?' there is nothing I could point to. I couldn't even discuss it in a tangible way. The shackles just dissipated, dissolved.

Nothing has changed except my perspective, my vision, the way I see it. I was, I am, and I will be ...something I like. It's not a case of turning myself into something good, but realising that the good has always been there, the fundamentals of self."

Next day I am walking the trails along the ridge behind where I live. I treasure this hour of quiet solitude. The view west to the Brindabella Mountains is vast, beyond the Murrumbidgee River that winds its way behind the foothills. The river's drunken path is revealed as a misty serpent, lazing translucent in the first rays of sunlight. You have to be up early to catch the wonder. Dwell too long over breakfast and you could not imagine such a sight was ever here.

Ideas flow when I'm out walking. I am intrigued by Darren's phrase, 'the fundamentals of self.' It sounds a long way from feeling depressed. Darren is saying what is fundamental to him now is a state of acceptance, an inner goodness where belonging and feeling loved is a birthright. These are the fundamentals that hold us together and enable us to flourish.

Darren's mention of the fundamentals of life is a first in many respects. It is personal, a recognition of who he is and what he has always been. His eyes have caught the glint, he can sense the goodness. The emotional trauma that had broken him has been significantly defused and there is a coming together of the precious human self. It is not a mechanical reconstruction of bits and pieces, but something far more mysterious. Darren is feeling more whole, more comfortable, his life is flowing. While his story is unusual, it is by no means unique.

Following the suicide of his mother and a marriage breakdown, the brilliant theoretical scientist, Wolfgang Pauli, fell into a deep personal crisis. The two years of therapy he spent with the famous psychologist, Carl Jung, are now folklore. Both men were profoundly influenced by their encounter and their relationship continued for years after the therapy ceased. Sometime later, in 1945, Pauli was awarded the Nobel Prize for contributions to quantum physics.

From a personal perspective, the therapy appears to have been very successful. Two years after starting therapy, Jung's assessment was that, "he did not drink anymore, he became completely adapted and in every respect completely normal."[61] Pauli remarried and this time the partnership lasted for the rest of his life.

Pauli had a great memory for dreams and he described several hundred over the course of therapy and in his later correspondences. Some of the dreams appeared to be related to his earlier life, while some reflected aspects of his therapy with Jung; others were related to his theoretical work. Jung discussed symbolism with Pauli, but made no attempt to interpret these dreams, allowing the dreamer to make of them what he would. At first Pauli resisted the idea of any connection between his scientific work and the content of his dreams. Later, however, he came to appreciate the relationship between certain dream imagery and his complex theories. More than this, he found the imagery in his dreams added depth and greater perspective to his theoretical knowledge.

Pauli wrote to Jung about the influence his dreams had on his work:

> "I gradually came to acknowledge that such fantasies or dreams are neither meaningless nor purely arbitrary, but rather convey a sort of second meaning of the terms applied."[62]

Pauli was working with some of the most complex ideas ever known and while he was sleeping, his inner mind converted that information into a pictorial form, giving it a 'sort of second meaning.' His unconscious mental activity didn't just 'understand' such complexities, it absorbed their implications and re-coded them into a different format that added meaning. Pauli's dreams were not mere copies of his theories, this was not just a memory being re-presented. By providing a 'second meaning' to his theories, Pauli's unconscious was demonstrating extraordinary intelligence in a seemingly effortless way.

The weaving together of reason and second meaning gives rise to new heights of understanding. Pauli referred to his 'outer mind' and his 'inner mind,' later using the terms 'quantitative' and 'symbolic.' The same mental duality is recognised by Professor Russell Meares as 'logical' and 'analogical,' both of which are essential for growth and wellbeing. Meares' use of 'analogical' is pertinent and deliberate.[63] An analogue resembles another thing, but it is not a copy. There is something added, bestowing new perspectives. When something is just a copy there can be no growth, nothing new. For Meares, it is this extraordinary analogical capacity of our inner mind, in reverberation with our logical mind that is fundamental to creativity and to the growth of self. Pauli's dreams were the manifestation of a new perspective on his logical thinking. The therapy with Jung helped Pauli re-integrate his previously fractured mind, giving voice to the creative genius and the fundamentals of self.

It is our memories that tell us who we are and where we have come from; they colour our moods and determine our decisions. The stories and the feelings they conjure up in us have taught us everything we know about ourselves. When trauma fractures our memories, we in turn, are diminished. Darren is right: what we need from therapy is to restore wholeness. Not to be changed, but to unfold into ever greater aspects of selfhood.

Imagery, metaphor, feelings and dreams are the language of the right brain. To be wowed by music, be inspired by a Shakespeare sonnet, or captivated by a sunrise; these are right brain dominant experiences. Like love, they cannot be described using reason, they cannot be measured. In contrast, logic is born out of the left side of our brain. Thinking, reasoning, rational deductions are all left brain dominant functions. Science is built upon the primacy of logic.

Even when our primary mode is logic, the use of metaphor and simile makes for clearer communication. Albert Einstein is said to have pictured himself sitting on a light beam travelling through space, imagery that set him on the path to formulating his astonishing theories. Wolfgang Pauli drew upon both a quantitative mind and a symbolic mind to realise his genius. In both these examples, the full potential of their endeavour could only be expressed using a balance of left and right brain involvement.

Darren finds himself in new territory with no idea how he arrived here. His quantitative mind is no longer over-analysing and questioning his every move. There is more involvement with his inner, symbolic mind. He is still getting used to feeling relief and release. He equates his new state with not trying so hard, not making lists, not setting goals, just going with the flow for a while. A return to balance. He does not know this part of himself, it has been lost for so long. His big fear is that he will lose it again, end up back where he was. To guard against this, he is super keen not to revert to previous ideas of trying to change himself. The word 'change' represents everything he was doing or trying to do previously that added to his torment.

"I baulk at the concept of 'changing how I feel.' Change brings in the issue of conscious control. I haven't changed, it's more that I've got to the point where the bad feelings aren't there. It's the feeling of letting go; feeling liberated. I don't see it as a change. I am aware some things have disappeared — like fear of failure, not being good enough, a lack of value, feeling worthless, etc. I used to use the word 'change' so much. I was so shit; there was so much I had to change about me. Now I recognise that I am fundamentally a good person. Acceptance of self is big for me, very important."

I understand what Darren has been trying to tell me; he is right. Working with subconscious therapy requires that we give up trying to change ourselves. When we let go and stop trying, it leaves space for the inner processes to do their healing work. The kinder, more loving thoughts that came to Darren during meditation emanated from his subconscious, just as the dream images of quantum physics came to Pauli from his subconscious. Therapy was the catalyst for both Pauli and Darren to become more whole, not to change. For both, in their very different ways, it was a greater wholeness, a greater synergy that gave voice to a combination of inner and outer mind. The resultant flow of creativity and healing is available for us all.

Darren has stopped talking. I sense there is more to come, so I wait. The long pause is testing, too often I jump in to avoid the awkwardness of silence. Darren isn't feeling awkward, not at all.

"I have to decide whether to continue therapy," he says.

"OK." I'm surprised, curious. "You're going well. Are you feeling confident you can manage on your own?"

"Things are going ok; symptoms have eased," he says. "But that isn't the reason why I'm reluctant to go on. I've reached a point where I'm comfortable enough and I don't have to go further. There is comfort in my current identity and a fear of the unknown if I continue. I wonder how attached I am to the security of being a sick person, an invalid pensioner? This has been my identity for so long. More than that, continuing on may reveal things about me I can't control. The crucial question is, what if I don't like who I am?"

This is brutally honest. Acknowledging he might not want a full recovery can feel weird, even shameful. I notice the question Darren poses is, 'What if I don't like who I am?' It's not, 'What if I don't like who I become?' How scary this is for someone emerging from a lifetime of self-loathing; quite different to the idea of therapy as a change agent. Implicit in being changed is the ability to change again if you don't like what you've become. But to be revealed, this is who you are, and if you don't like it, tough, this is you for all time. As Darren says, "Once you know it, you can't un-know it."

He continues, "I was always able to control the conversation before (with talk therapy). With this approach it's different. I'm not in control, at least not in the same way. Finishing therapy now would be a compromise, I know that. There could be more improvement to come, but exactly what that is, or what will emerge, I have no idea."

Darren's dilemma is accentuated by his fear of the unknown and a determination to be true to himself. He also has a stubborn refusal to do anything half hearted. He could settle for where he is now. Or he could re-commit to furthering the healing process; to explore what else there is to know about himself.

"My years of depression have left me without sunlight, not nurtured; entangled in weeds and briars. Therapy is gradually pulling out a few weeds and letting the sun in, allowing a few green shoots and even a little blossom. I am not changing, but the flower is being allowed out. Now I am wondering what kind of flower I am."

Once Darren starts getting flowery with me, I know what his decision will be. His right brain paints pictures. His left brain fears uncertainty. Right brain wins. Darren thinks it over for a couple of weeks, then decides he will continue with therapy. I am unsure how much more I can help, but that does not seem to concern him.

In the meditation that follows, I return to a much earlier theme. The same words, more or less, but he is so much softer now; he has different ears. Sometimes good dinner conversations can be sparked by the question: 'What advice would you give to your eight year old self?' Therapy brings a similar idea into the clinic room. It is known as inner child work. When used in conjunction with meditative trance and storytelling, it is surprisingly emotive. I introduce Darren's younger self near the end of the meditation:

> "...Now let the present Darren turn to that younger Darren, at whatever age he is when those feelings are first felt. The part of you who's been holding on tight such a long time... not able to smile perhaps for a long time.
>
> Look into his face, look into his eyes... Find a way to comfort him, to reassure him... Let him know how much you admire him... because you know he's always done the best he could... as though he were your only child, let him know that he's loved

— deeply loved... Not so much for anything he might do or not do... he doesn't have to earn the love...it's his birthright...always was, always will be... loved...loved for being who he is...a unique, beautiful expression of life... No one else in all the world will ever express life the way he does. That's how special he is, how precious...

Take a moment of private time to be with him... Hold him against you, feel the warmth of his body and the beat of his heart... He's real, as real as you are... listen to his fears and his needs... his longings... So he feels heard and understood... nurtured...cherished...he feels worthy ...cherished... he belongs... he is safe... ..."

Months later Darren is doing well. "What's changed?" I ask, expecting a reaction to the word, but there is none. He tells me,

"I'm peaceful, a place I've never been before. Things aren't locked up any more, everything's open for gentle looking at." After a long pause Darren continues.

"What this therapy has done for me is like an exercise in optometry. It has allowed me to view a whole range of different aspects of myself. I feel an excitement, satisfaction and happiness, where previously there was only dark shades of grey. This has widened the scope of vision for me and allowed the colour through. The window is still the same; the eyes have changed."

'The eyes have changed.' How curious. This is changing from the inside, seeing life through different eyes. However much Darren wanted to get better, nothing really changed until he stopped pushing, until he could allow the shackles to dissolve. He does not fear discovering who he is anymore; more than ever he recognises in himself the fundamentals that have always been there.

A few years ago I became crippled and could barely walk. I needed a hip replacement. Good fortune came in the form of a great surgeon. His name is Dr Alexander Burns and, as far as I am concerned, he is the best in the business. He said he would charge me, but he never said he would change me. Six weeks later I was walking around with very little pain, feeling lighter and freer and much relieved. I have the precious gift of mobility again, I can walk for hours, I'm less cranky, but I haven't changed. From the start Dr Burns had a clear picture of the final outcome. In therapy, however, I seldom do.

I confide to Darren, "At no stage did I ever come close to imagining how you would be, how you are now." He replies straight back:

"That says a lot about this therapy. There was no pre-determined destination. You were never trying to turn me into something 'normal' in your eyes. You were trying to help me release the real me. This has been about releasing, unshackling, unchaining; setting me free. It was never about 'converting' or 'normalising.' You didn't build a trellis and wind me through it and say, grow this way."

Mental wellbeing and personal therapy can open us up to that which is unchangeable. Healing ultimately involves revealing ourselves, uncovering what is real within us. As the poet Rumi says, "You who are not naked yet, you can go back to sleep."[64]

Chapter 13

The Halfway House

" like a lot of me — even the things that cause me grief. I catch myself saying things I wasn't aware of." The old hesitation is gone, so is the Bob Hawke eye roll. Darren is in the flow.

"In some respects I understand less about myself now than I did before. I'm learning to live again, learning how to be comfortable with uncertainty and surprise... Before, I would analyse and analyse and come up with a position. Now I can just be a streamer in the wind, that's how I hear myself... I describe my feelings using analogy on analogy; like a boat without moorings, like taking to the old side roads off the main highway, like pulling out weeds so the flowers could grow. Picture book descriptions; I have no cognitive understanding of how these changes have occurred."

Darren may forget all this by next week, so I write furiously, scrambling to capture the moment.

"Where did that come from?" He pauses. "These conversations are like a halfway-house between meditation and normal consciousness, it opens a window to my subconscious. I say things before I've even thought of them." I tear off another page of writing and Darren slows down for me. Despite my scribbling frenzy, I am fully engaged.

"When I first came here, if something wasn't logical, it wasn't real. Over time I've come to notice I am tapping into something different. There is cognitive involvement, but not cognitive control. Emotional input is allowed. That's unusual. There's this middle ground where emotional feelings and attitudes are verbalised. The halfway house feels a bit like a transit lounge, like I'm on a journey where two parts of me are coming together. But it's an ongoing journey, I'm not there yet."

Two parts coming together. The old, logical, over-analysing self and this new self, less restricted, open to his emotional nature. Which one is the real Darren? Whichever one he inhabits at the time. There is no doubt that this latest Darren is preferable; he likes himself, he is spontaneous, flowing and more able to express feelings.

Darren's Mum has been staying with him for a few days. His Mum is elderly and practically blind. I ask him, "How has it been?"

"The last two weeks with Mum have been very different. I was anticipating the old me. I expected to feel pressured, exposed and checked upon. What I experienced was the flow of relationship, conversation rather than interrogation, sharing rather than exposure, observation rather than scrutiny. Mum said I was a lot more open about things and she didn't have to interrogate me."

I am no longer waiting for Darren to finish sentences; he is waiting for me to catch up. It seems as though everything he says is fresh, a stream of consciousness bubbling up from an inner spring.

"It was really important to me that I do this well. It was a big thing this time. I didn't feel I was a sick person doing my best; I felt I was a competent adult doing what I wanted. I don't know that I've ever felt that before... "

"But it's funny, it's not an effort. It's like the whole intensity of living has decreased, leaving a mixture of relaxed appreciation and wonderment. Like being in the country, seeing the ocean or the rolling hills — a quiet contentment. I'm not going to get excited about being better now. I'm coming at this from an entirely different angle. It's a state I never knew existed; I never knew this is how you lived." I nod encouragingly and he continues.

"It's like being driven somewhere blindfolded, then taking the blindfold off. This is different; I'm not excited about getting here, because I never knew where here was. All I know is that it's a nicer place to be; interesting to watch my spirit come out of me in this new environment. In some ways I'm too busy observing me to get excited. There are not too many opportunities in life to see myself for the first time."

I don't say anything, happy to let the flow continue, offering the occasional 'uh-huh.'

"The last two weeks have been an epitome of that. I've had a responsibility: it's been up to me to take care of Mum. It's been a long time since I haven't been scared by that. There used to be hours of torturous analysis of what was next and how I should do this and that. Normally I'd be complying with a whole set of self-imposed rules. That's what I was anticipating. Lo and behold, she arrives and it's like we go into a theatre and there's a movie playing. Gone is the constant monitoring — the questioning, 'is this right?' I'm concerned about things, yes, but without being weighed down by the treacle of self-examination and second guessing. Yes, I'm just in the breeze now — not the treacle..."

I tear off another page. These notes are precious because at our next session Darren may not feel this way, nor remember what he has been saying. Not until I read his words back to him. The notes capture the moment. These halfway house moments had their origins earlier in our therapy. Occasions when Darren was genuinely surprised to hear the extent of his own self-hatred. Back then he reflected:

"I'm seeing all this venom and disdain; the hard-core belief in my victimhood. I am shocked by it; I can't understand it. It scares me how much hate there is, the level of venom. Even I don't hate myself as much as these words do." Later, in the midst of more vitriol, he suddenly announced, 'That's not right, that's not fair!' These were entrees into Darren's world of unconscious thought. Now we are into the main course.

Our sessions always begin with time for talking; often about the trivia of life; shared sporting interests, or a recent television program. The trivial develops into the personal and occasionally, like today, he is different and something is let loose. Today his voice is upbeat, not the usual monotone and this is what captures me; it is compulsive listening. It has strength and dignity.

"It is clear to me," Darren says, reflecting on his lack of recall of our halfway house conversations, "I was speaking from another source. That was the reason I had no memory. *I wasn't there, not in a cognitive involvement sense.* It was so different for me; previously every experience had to be vetted consciously and carefully sanitised before it could be spoken."

Darren continues, his voice increasingly certain, "I didn't recognise what was happening at the time. It was later when we read the notes that I became aware I had been talking from a different source. One that didn't seem to have the same ability to be recalled."

"But you recognised they were your words?" I ask.

"I had a vague memory, enough to know I wasn't being verballed." He says. "It's weird, very different to other therapies I've done. Like there's this fermentation period following weeks of our sessions. Then the words come out when the subconscious is ready. But it's only because I am comfortable here. This place feels like a safe haven for me; it's allowed an opening up so I can tap into that other source."

Darren is giving voice to his unconscious. He appears to have access into mental processes before they reach conscious awareness. He finds himself describing ideas he had never previously known. He questions, 'where did that come from?' He is genuinely incredulous, yet he knows it is his voice, his mind, offering a brief glimpse of the unconscious healing incubating inside him.

There are more insights over the next few weeks; I write them down and read them back to him at the following session and, of course, he has forgotten. These cycles of revelation, forgetting and re-minding are unlike anything I have known before. Darren is convinced much of his recent improvement is due not only to these halfway house conversations, but also to hearing his words read back to him; bearing witness to his emerging self.

I have always understood that a period of subconscious incubation is necessary for successful therapy. Witnessing these subconscious processes made explicit is a rare and privileged insight into the creative genius of the mind.

The incubation effect is a part of folklore, with many famous examples from history. When the renowned French mathematician Henri Poincaré arrived at the solution to a problem that had troubled him for years, he reportedly exclaimed, "The idea came to me without anything in my former thoughts seeming to have paved the way for it."[65] A master of reason, Poincaré had no logical explanation of where his flash of insight had come from. Not everyone is a mathematical genius, but many of us have experienced an 'aha' moment, a solution springing to mind from seemingly nowhere.

In 2009, Professor Allan Snyder and his team from Sydney University published research demonstrating the non-conscious generation of ideas in a group of volunteers.[66] The research explores the links between the creative process and problem solving. Participants were asked open ended questions like, 'How many uses can you think of for a piece of paper?' There was a characteristic burst of ideas that trailed off after five minutes, at which point the participants were told the exercise was over. They were then asked to do a different exercise for ten minutes before they were unexpectedly returned to the first problem. All participants then had a burst of further ideas that subsequently trailed off in a similar pattern to the first phase, indicating a subliminal incubation of fresh ideas had occurred between the two phases of the exercise. Interestingly, this happened even though the participants were told the exercise was over after the first phase.

A similar period of incubation lies at the core of P.S.H. therapy. Stories heard in trance trigger a series of subliminal processes that, over time, generate new feelings and experiences. The incubation period after a P.S.H. session can vary in length from ten minutes, to overnight, to 10 days, often more in Darren's case.

However, incubation does not always lead to successful hatching. Many ideas that form in the subconscious mind do not survive the journey into our conscious awareness. There can be many reasons for the process stalling. Our nervous system can be overwhelmed by the daily events of life — traumatic situations where Darren saw his health problems as life threatening, or when events threatened the wellbeing of his daughter. Nor can life enhancing ideas develop in a toxic emotional environment. Like the parable of the sower and the seed, new thoughts and feelings must fall on good soil and be carefully tended and nurtured in order to flourish. Darren's burst of positive thoughts and ideas is possible now because so much of his emotional baggage has dissolved.

We are often unwilling to credit our unconscious mind for the amazing work it performs. I am eternally grateful to the human genius and skill that gave me a hip replacement, but I recognise that once my operation was over, there was a lot of healing to be done. Intelligent, creative healing, beneath the staples, adapting to and adopting the alien prosthesis that restored my mobility. Darren's wounds are less physical (although his cardio-vascular system is collateral damage) but the principle remains. His healing is a non-conscious process, for at his core he is a self-organising, self-healing and self-generating being. While I am there to assist, there can be no doubt that the healing function is happening within him, *yet without* his conscious control. A startling paradox emerges; we need the presence of, and interaction with, a caring other to enable this intensely personal healing to occur. While the therapist engages in an active way, she must relinquish any need to control the outcome and allow the healing function to unfold in its own unique way. The healing function is outside of *all* conscious control.

When we drop off to sleep at night, we hand over responsibility for our life to our unconscious processes, assured that we will wake up again in the morning. Throughout the night the unconscious mind is restoring and healing mind and body. Come the morning, we step into another day without a thought for the amazing transformation that has occurred inside us. It is as if we go off to bed leaving the kitchen a mess of used pots and dirty dishes, then in the morning, through blurry eyes, seeing that all is cleaned up and put away in its place once more.

Unfortunately, we are a culture where the need for conscious control dominates and there is little respect for the organising and healing processes occurring inside us. No coincidence that we are a society increasingly sleep deprived.

I am in Sydney attending a psychotherapy seminar. The speaker is the English psychiatrist and psychoanalyst, Dr Jean Knox, a leading voice in modern psychotherapy. By coincidence, my brother recently sent me a copy of her latest book, so I have a good sense of what she will be presenting.[67] There is a large turnout and I arrive just in time to claim one of the few vacant chairs. My head is fuzzy from the four hour drive and pre-dawn start. Looking around the room, there are no familiar faces among the murmuring chatter. I give a nod to the person sitting next to me, then the seminar starts with an acknowledgement of the Gadigal people, the traditional custodians of the place we now call Sydney.

By morning break I have an aching need for coffee and food that overrides the niceties of meeting new people. Conveniently I forget the caffeine-free diet I have been on for several months. I perch myself on my own in the corner, juggling cup and saucer and cake-on-a-plate in shaking hands (that's the caffeine), feeling a little more human, although a lot like Michael-no-friends. The first session was interesting and I have taken a liking to this speaker. The subject is 'developing self-agency in therapy.' There is warmth and wisdom as Dr Knox relates case histories and backgrounds her theories. Certain people I meet in these settings are so comfortable in themselves and in their expertise that they do not need to sound clever. They are not selling. They simply come with a genuine desire to teach and share their truth. Dr Knox strikes me in this way and I am grateful.

The idea of self-agency is complex and there are a number of theories that feed into our understanding, from attachment theory to neuroscience. It is one of those things, you know it when you see it — or rather feel it. Except that is not a thing, nor a destination, but a constantly changing flow, influenced by daily events and our interactions with others. All the more confusing for there are many impersonators, many who sound confident. Charismatic personalities who swagger and mock in their desperate need for control and power. They are the antithesis of self-agency; their self-aggrandizement is a façade to cover disowned terror and shame. Such is the nature of the human condition that these people often appear successful, rising to great heights as leaders in politics, business, media or religion. No names needed, I'm sure you will recognise one or two as you listen to the news in the morning.

In contrast, it seems to me that Dr Knox is an exemplar of comfortable self-agency as she talks and engages with the group. The ideas she is presenting are not new to me. Nothing new, and yet something is added. Self-agency means knowing we have the capacity to act and shape our environment, while respecting the legitimate self-agency of others. The topic leads me back to thoughts of Darren. His childhood and adolescence were characterised by an impotence to prevent his father's descent into alcoholism. This learned 'failure' would be repeated later as his tried unsuccessfully to lift his wife out of her post-natal depression and to save their marriage, while simultaneously unable to achieve basic outcomes at work. He felt incompetent as a father. The repeated feelings of frustration and failure resulted in an impoverished sense of self-agency and became major contributors to Darren's growing anxiety and depression.

In contrast, the recent halfway house conversations are a convincing display of growing self-agency. He talks of liking himself and of being less concerned with what others think of him. There is still work to be done, but these are signs of a huge transformation taking place inside him.

Suddenly aware Dr Knox is continuing her talk, I struggle to catch where the discussion is up to, quickly checking around and making sure I have not become the object of attention during my brief dissociation from the room. Relieved to find my anonymity intact, I give Dr Knox my full attention. The talk has turned to a recent model of learning and development, as proposed by Professor Annette Karmiloff-Smith.[68] It is a model where learning begins and develops at an unconscious level, emerging into consciousness over a period of time, ultimately reaching the state where it can be verbalised. I find it curiously coincidental that I should be hearing this right now. It explains a lot about the incubation effect and Darren's halfway house conversations. At home the following day, I look up Professor Karmiloff-Smith's book, 'Beyond Modularity' and delve deeper into her theory. It is complex and I find the language testing, but it is definitely worth the effort. Karmiloff-Smith is describing Darren's experience to a tee.

It is a 3-phase model that develops simultaneously across different domains of knowledge. Development occurs independently domain by domain. For example, musical intelligence develops separately to maths or science.

During the first phase, learning is externally sourced; different forms of information, or experience (e.g. attending a seminar, learning to surf, or listening to a story) are received through our various senses and collated together with previous learnings; there is little interconnection or tailoring with what is already known. It is not yet integrated, just a collection of different experiences. Inevitably, there can be apparent contradictions or inconsistencies at this stage.

In the second phase, the focus of learning switches to an internally driven *re-presentation* of experiences, where different areas of the brain re-code the information and make links with previous memories in the same domain of knowledge. Individual impressions are edited, added to, or relinquished as learning develops toward a coherent, interconnected body of knowledge. This complex and highly intelligent operation happens entirely beneath our conscious threshold; the basis of all learning, we would literally be lost without it.

During the third phase, the process of representing and re-coding information continues. Karmiloff-Smith explains:

"...internal representations and external data are reconciled and a balance is achieved between the quests for internal and external control."[69]

Knowledge becomes more conscious; there are thoughts and feelings that straddle the conscious-unconscious divide. The final stage of the learning process is achieved when re-coding converts information into a conscious form that can be verbalised.

Karmiloff-Smith emphasises that information undergoes a period of incubation as it proceeds through stages of unconscious knowing, before emerging into conscious awareness as thought or activity:

'...a process by which implicit information *in* the mind subsequently becomes explicit knowledge *to* the mind.'[70]

She notes there can be times when the natural order of the incubation process changes and knowledge moves directly from the subconscious to verbalisation before becoming conscious. That is the final piece, the clincher. Karmiloff-Smith's model now fits precisely with Darren's halfway house experience.

Darren's unconscious re-coding of our meditation sessions had proceeded unseen for weeks. Neither of us were privy to what was being processed, until suddenly, Darren began talking about himself in a whole new way. This new sense of himself emerged directly from his unconscious, surprising Darren and leading him to question, "Where did that come from?" Verbal access to his unconscious was, I imagine, prompted by the feel and atmosphere of the clinic room, relaxed and uninhibited and where he was familiar with taking journeys into his inner world.

Our halfway house conversations are remarkably consistent. Themes are congruent, repeating and looping back to other themes discussed months earlier. This is important to Darren, an integrity issue. Previously, his inner critic edited every thought, every word. Now, for these brief interludes, the inner critic is silent. He talks without pausing to think; "I like a lot of me — even the things that cause me grief." Can he believe what he hears? The ongoing consistency of these conversations proves to Darren that he can trust his subconscious self; he concludes these experiences are genuine.

Trust in himself is critical. Previously Darren was reluctant to speak positively about his progress, for fear of building hope that might be dashed. His past was littered with failed attempts to get better and each failure hurt him more. Upon hearing his words now, he does not recoil from their sentiments of warm positive regard for himself, nor does he beat himself up for being arrogant, or self-centred like he did in the past. Instead they are pinned to the mast; an important step in establishing ownership and a marker on his journey of recovery.

"I woke up this morning feeling happy — I've not had that feeling for such a long time. It was a noticeably different feeling. I wanted to get up and do things, be engaged with life. The most exciting part of it was I kept asking myself, 'What am I happy about?' And I kept hearing me answer, 'nothing in particular.' That's really exciting. That's the closest I can come to describing the absence of depression; to observe myself being happy about nothing in particular, but just feeling happy, naturally..."

This feeling was unimaginable before. The regenerative capacities of our mind are astonishing, way beyond anything our brightest intellect could command. After 20 years of unrelenting depression, Darren now feels whole; at this moment he is happy in himself without needing anything external to feel happy about.

In the past an artist would paint over a previous work, possibly to save it from destruction from religious zealots, or simply because she/he could not afford another canvas. Centuries later the original painting is discovered by an art expert and lovingly restored; its over-paint carefully dissolved and the essential genius fully recognised. Darren is both restorer and restored. After a lifetime of hiding away, his unique self is emerging. A masterpiece recovered; the essential nature of mind.

Healing The Mind That Can't Let Go

Chapter 14

The Emerging Self

Darren has an appointment at the Tax Department.

He has sorted out his papers and is engaging with life again; the daily things he could not face before. After living a third of his life with depression, he has some serious catching up to do.

"Is there anyone here who can help me with my returns?" he asks.

An officer leads the way to an interview room. Small, non-descript, grey carpet, plain desk, a familiar office smell. It is a typical city office building, similar to where he worked for many years and where he was subjected to humiliation and bullying. Normally he avoids such places. It was a similar building where he attended an interview with an independent psychiatrist, who determined the extent of compensation for his work-related trauma. Even before he met the psychiatrist, just entering the building triggered a rapid heart rate, sweaty palms and a mental blank. This is brave.

"Good morning, sir. Which tax year are we dealing with?" asks the tax officer.

"Last year's," replies Darren.

"No problem. I expect we can give you an extension of time for lodgement," says the tax officer.

"Er, last 14 years, actually," says Darren.

"I see. Well let's start with last year and work backwards." Dispelling the stereotypes, the tax officer is compassionate, taking time to explain the various requirements for all the years and outlining a series of lodgement dates. All up, Darren has three months.

Four months and another two visits later, all the returns are lodged. A pay-by-the-month plan is agreed. Darren is pleased despite the financial pain. I ask him,

"Did they know you've been sick?"

Darren is not sure. "That might be why they haven't come for me before now."

Next is an appointment with the dentist, his first in over a decade. It confirms the worst. His teeth aren't just black, they are rotten. The lower set are taken out first. The dentures take a while to get comfortable. I switch from multigrain to wholemeal bread and cut the crusts off his toast. When the pain subsides he gets the upper set done. This time the discomfort lasts longer, but he manages the pain. He can smile at himself in the mirror now.

These are significant achievements for someone who has had long term depression; they required sustained energy and commitment over time. Darren was not coached into doing these things, nor did he discuss them with me beforehand. They are an expression of self-agency; his belief in himself and his ability to get things done. I understand why Jean Knox rates self-agency as a vital aspect of successful therapy. Interestingly though, it was never targeted during our therapy, there were no strategies plotted, yet self-agency has emerged and here is Darren taking charge of his life.

Recovery has taken time, but it is no less remarkable for that. The fog and treacle of depression that had engulfed him for years disappeared a few weeks after therapy began, only to be replaced by heightened feelings of anxiety. There were ups and downs, but Darren kept turning up at my clinic, regardless of how he was feeling. He kept turning up through the long months when nothing seemed to change. He kept turning up. He has been free of depressive episodes for over three years. His relationship with his children has developed well beyond what he thought possible. He talks with them most days. There was always love, but that gets confused in the presence of anxiety and despair. Kindness and patience have replaced guilt and fear. His focus is on learning to live again.

Our talks invariably include comparisons of how Darren's life is now, as opposed to how it was before. This 'before and after' contrast never ceases to amaze us and we discuss the idea of writing a book about his journey. At first just a joke or two, 'that would make a good chapter heading!' Later the talk gets more serious. Darren is keen:

"It's like some stories need to be told. Particularly stories of hope where the subject is a problem that so many people suffer from."

Ideas grow and we make a list of major themes to be included. I have many folders of session notes to draw from, including pages of Darren talking, recorded word for word. My first job will be to start typing up these notes — a daunting task for my two finger typing style. Covering certain parts of the journey will be harrowing for Darren, recalling the darkest times, but he insists he is OK. Perhaps this will be a final purging of his demons. We take it slowly, setting aside times for writing in an interview style. We sit in the kitchen — not the clinic room — and I dress casually.

Darren talks about his children more than ever. They are part of his story and are well placed to observe his recovery. Their feedback is affirming. "Dad seems so Zen these days, just laid back, and doesn't get perturbed, like Buddha!"

"That's Renee, my youngest daughter," says Darren. "And it's interesting, I find I don't have to be overtly happy to be happy."

I ask Darren for permission to talk with Renee about her experiences of her Dad. It seems relevant to the story. He is fine about it.

"It's OK that he fucked up," she says with a twinkle. "I like that he owns it — he'll talk about it, so honest. It gives me more empathy for others, especially those with mental illness. I'm impressed at how he's turned it around, put in the time. It's very inspiring when people fuck up that bad and turn it around. Makes me feel secure. I think, if I fuck up it'll be OK. Takes the fear out of failing. I really appreciate that he respects me enough to be honest, to admit that he made mistakes. He just did what he could at the time. That's how I feel, impressed."

Darren's eldest daughter, Grace, describes him this way:

"He's not just my Dad, we're good friends and I trust him. He's able to live without the tangles of the spider's web, no longer thinking about what he thinks, what others think, going over situations, rehashing, beating himself up. Just being able to say what he thinks, regardless. I can have a real conversation; he has energy now, not worn out on the treadmill. Now he speaks from his insides."

Grace has known her dad through the depths of his depression. She can remember him from when she was very young.

"When Dad recalls how unwell he was, the viciousness of his self-loathing, it's like I'm looking back, almost from above. I can see myself, feeling the hatred, embarrassment, shame, the not good enough. That's a bit scary."

"Growing up, Dad was strict. I didn't dare push it. But then he was such fun, exuberant, clever. He made me think. I remember him like that. All this energy and enthusiasm, then total collapse, nothing, empty, he was gone, shut down. The fun got less and less. He was gone more and more. Worse and worse, he would stay away at the club. Someone so close getting further and further away. I was 10, 11 years old."

I am aware of repeated patterns, parallels with Darren and his own dad.

"When he and Mum split up, I went with him. He was always saying, 'I gotta get my shit together and try harder, effort, effort, effort,' then he'd collapse. I lived with him for a year before being put into foster care. I'd go along and watch him at sports training being brave, putting on a performance for the kids. It took a huge amount of effort for him, staying in control, then afterwards he had nothing left. But I think the training kept him alive."

"How was it when your Dad started getting better?" I ask.

Grace shakes her head. "Dad getting better makes me realise how hard it was back then. Change was a trickle to begin with. Early on my fear was 'will this last?' I was always on edge, ready to catch him when he fell. He was so hard on himself before, always a feeling of not being good enough. Now he's putting himself in the picture, that's really new."

"We know he's there for all of us, no matter what. That's lovely. He tells me he feels loved by everyone. Before he wouldn't let it in — it was just words. Lately he tells me how much he likes himself, that's so nice to hear. It's one of those things I always wished for. I just wanted him to see what I saw. There wasn't anything I wouldn't do to get him to see what I and others saw in him."

"Before it was a case of everything needed to be fixed and he needed to fix it. To a large extent that is gone, replaced by an acceptance. It's not his job to fix everyone, to fix the world. And he doesn't have to pay for his sins into eternity. That has helped our relationship. His demeanour now is even; more playful. He always had a unique sense of humour. Now it doesn't matter if anyone else laughs — that's hilarious!"

"Dad says the hard things with a bit more love these days. Before it was, 'what you need to do…' and 'someone needs to tell you…' Now it's become, 'you seem a bit wound up…' He gets me in with questions and stories, stories about himself. I see the same thing flowing through in his coaching."

"He's present, unedited. He is more flexible, doesn't get so frustrated. Such a privilege being a part of his journey. I just never know where it goes…Dad is gentle, soft and fair. I'm watching him be soft and gentle with himself now, and he's being fair to himself."

I am at the airport looking for something easy to read for the journey. My wife, Deb and I are travelling north for some winter sunshine, hoping to relax more and throw off the Canberra cold. The headline in the New Scientist grabs me, 'Is Humanity Getting More Stupid?' It's just the sort of distraction I need for the three and a half hour journey.

By the time the seatbelt sign is switched off, I have lost interest in the headline story. Another article, 'Dreams Act as Overnight Therapy,' has caught my attention. It is research showing how the content and intensity of our dreams is directly related to the intensity of our emotional experiences while we are awake. Not that surprising, really. The article describes how Mark Blagrove and his team at Swansea University devised clever experiments that prove this is the case.[71]

Dreams occur during Rapid Eye Movement (REM) sleep, when electrical activity in the brain oscillates between four and seven hertz, generating what is commonly known as theta waves. Volunteers wore electroencephalogram (EEG) caps that measured their brainwaves while they slept, so researchers could wake them when they were dreaming and record details of their dreams. Each participant kept a diary of their daily lives and these were compared to their dream records. Events that had a higher emotional impact were more likely to become incorporated into a person's dreams, suggesting that the most intense dreaming activity occurs when our subconscious is working hard to process emotionally powerful experiences.

"This is the first finding that theta waves are related to dreaming... and the strongest evidence yet that dreaming is related to the processing that the brain is doing of recent memories," said Blagrove. "If dreams do act as a sort of overnight therapy to sooth the emotional impact of our experiences, it raises the prospect of manipulating our sleeping brains to improve this process."[72] Blagrove suggests it may be possible to hack our dreams and one way to do this would be to drive brainwaves into theta frequency using sound.

Many of our dreams are stories, told by our unconscious mind while we are in a theta brain state, in order to de-potentiate the emotional impact of previous experiences. The parallels with P.S.H. therapy are clear. P.S.H. also seeks to de-potentiate the emotional impact of past events by telling stories while the client is in deep meditation — also a theta brain state. It provides a gentle approach that works with and facilitates the natural processes of 'overnight therapy.' Carefully crafted stories mimic the effect of dreaming and particular use of voice promotes deep relaxation. Once again, it is heartening to find modern research that supports the P.S.H. approach.

Stepping out at Cairns airport, the tropical air is an instant balm. We head for the hire car in high spirits.

Darren continues to see me. Increasingly he is freed-up, mellow, feeling comfortable in the presence of uncertainty and able to express a wide range of emotions. I am witnessing the emergence of his real self, in constant flux, unburdened and released from his past. He seems more open to daily interactions with family, his few friends, the kids he trains and their families. This is the precious human self, intimate and ineffable, vulnerable to trauma just like the physical body and with the same capacity for healing and self-generation. Darren talks openly about his family life:

"I'm enjoying time with Matthew, my (nine month old) grandson, feeling wonderful when he lies on my chest, close to the heart beat. Energising. But all is not well here. He has problems with his hearing and sight. I feel a protective response — not the head worry, more a heart response. I'm feeling sad about this today, but despite that, it is nice to realise I've got to the point where I can be touched, where my heart can feel touched. I'm proud that I didn't trade my identity to get here. Nice to be able to feel like this — sadness, rooted in love. Wanting to pick up Alison (Matthew's Mum) and Matty and hold them and hold them. Sad as all buggery, but it's a lovely feeling and I didn't have that before." Clearing his throat, he continues.

"This dispels the illusion that depression is a sadness, it's the absence of sadness. A prerequisite for sadness is an ability to feel. My depression was an inability to feel, a vacuum, a black hole, an overabundance of nothingness. I can only say that it is nice to feel this sadness that hurts like buggery, because I know what a vacuum feels like."

There is progress elsewhere in his life.

"I've been announcing my birthday coming up. In the past I would go to great lengths not to tell anyone. 'Don't make a fuss about me.' I hated any fuss. It is the first time in a great many years — highly significant because it's happening outside the clinic room. I'm moving from the clinic room to 'out there.' No effort involved, no plan, an impromptu manifestation of a different character."

"I seem less guarded talking to people about my history of depression, with people I trust," he says. "I don't worry about what they might think of me, less need to present an image... I told this friend about my depression and having these sessions with you. She seemed surprised. I said to her 'I'm the best I've ever been in my life.' I don't remember telling anyone that before and yet I'm thinking this feels normal to talk like this, I'm observing something normal."

Darren's emerging self is affecting his sports coaching.

"Parents are giving me nice feedback about my training, telling me what a good environment it is," he says. "The mix of ages, the supportive culture. They are happy to have their kids come and be there. I feel it's partly due to how I am. While those things have always been important to me, I'm not forcing it now. Numbers are up this month, the best for years."

Teaching kids to run, jump and play sport has been a big part of Darren's life. He often brings it up in our sessions, but now the talk is taking a different tone:

"I mixed the relay teams yesterday. The kids loved it. The parents could see how happy the 'littlies' were, mixing with the big boys and girls. It's not just the kids that are excited, playful, it's the parents too. It means a lot having the group interaction, seeing their kids coming out of themselves, watching their social skills develop. One kid used to sit some distance away from the group, but yesterday his Mum says to me, 'can't you just see how he's smiling.' Top stuff! The building blocks for the future..."

Darren regularly spends time with his two grandchildren at the local swimming centre. Even when he is tired, these times are highlights of his week. He tells me,

"Playing with Matty yesterday at the pool, it was lovely, he's getting to that interactive phase, just great!" In an aside, he says, "I'm getting a waviness in my eye, my good eye. It varies from day to day; not too bad at the moment."

Next week Darren reports his sleep is better. Most nights he is sleeping through until 5 am. This is encouraging. His poor sleep patterns are the final legacy of his depression. He adds, "My eye still gets that waviness."

As I open the door I know instantly today is not a good day. I was half expecting it. Recent tests have shown a deterioration in Darren's vision and his reading ability. The waviness prompted him to get a check-up and the news is that he may lose the sight in his one good eye. Over the years he had seen his mother become blind as she aged, so he knows what to expect. This is dry macular degeneration and it appears to be genetic. There is no cure. It is not associated with his mental illness. Except that this ranks pretty high on the scale of anxiety provoking events.

I fetch the coffee and toast, seeking the comfort of ritual.

Darren opens the conversation. "I'm not sure what's going on. I had another eye appointment two days ago and it's sent me into a spiral." This latest appointment was to test the state of his cataracts. It is a common operation to remove them.

"What's happened" I ask, "were the results bad?"

"No, I don't think so," he says. "This guy had a different way of testing, so I don't know what to think. These results showed no deterioration in the macular condition. But that's at odds with the previous tests and it doesn't explain why I still have this waviness going on. The guy didn't seem to have an answer. We did the reading test and there, too, it was more normal."

"This sounds like good news," I say.

"Yes, that's what Renee said when she drove me home from the hospital, but somehow it's drained every bit of energy out of me. Before, I thought I understood what was going on, now I'm confused, got no idea. I should be seeing this as good news, but for some reason, it doesn't cut it for me."

Two weeks ago Darren had found the prognosis around his eyesight upsetting. A natural response, given the circumstances. Now this latest news offers more hope, but Darren's reaction is actually more severe.

He continues, "Until this latest appointment I was managing my anxiety. I was constantly checking to see what I could see, but for the most part, I was pleased with the maturity of my response, the absence of catastrophising and self-pity. I've been open with the kids, whereas in the past I would have kept it all to myself. Now I don't know what to think anymore, it doesn't feel like good news, just more uncertainty. Uncertainty trumps good news any day."

Next week Darren is the same. "My confidence is rocked; I can't make decisions at sports training — I asked Trent to take over for me. I'm feeling angry. I'm panicking again over my health, checking every twinge, what's that pain? It's drop-kicked me back into a state I've not been in for a long time. I had a panic attack in the supermarket, felt my heart racing, feeling spacey. I had to get out of there…"

The implications of going blind could be devastating for any of us. Darren's reaction is commensurate with such a prognosis. Perversely, it has taken a second, more hopeful scenario for Darren to fully understand what he might lose. The uncertainty disrupts his defences. It is a cruel turn of events. I struggle to deal with the idea myself; not knowing what to say. Once more I fear his depression returning.

Unsure where it will lead, I guide Darren into a meditation. This is a different challenge now. The painful orphans of his past have largely been laid to rest. His future is less clear; the only certainty is that there will be loss. How can we prepare ourselves for such a prospect? He is well attuned to my meditation voice and relaxes deeply, despite his agitated state a few minutes ago. I am drawn intuitively to the guided meditations of Steven Levine and his exquisite themes of mercy and compassion. I select one he calls 'A Healing Shared in Loving Kindness.'[73]

We are 10 minutes into the meditation:

"...with each in-breath, whispering silently in your heart, 'may I be happy, may I be free of suffering, may I be at peace'...with each out-breath, 'may my pain be healed, may I enter the joy of my true nature, beyond even this longing to be free...

...Peace comes into the heart like the morning sun spreading across the ocean. It is the ocean of compassion. It is the bright light of mercy flooding the heart. Welling over into the body. The whole body softening in mercy and loving kindness..."

The practice of loving kindness comes in three expanding stages. The first stage is about ourselves, the second stage is about those we love and care for and the third stage is opening to embrace all sentient beings. The feeling of compassion is stirred in the heart, where it takes form as oxytocin and is pumped through our veins.

"...and recognising that just as you wish to be happy so do all beings everywhere; begin to send this healing kindness, this loving mercy out to another. Perhaps a dear friend ... a beloved person in your life ... touch them now. Send to them now this same wish for their wellbeing that you are absorbing into your body for your own deep healing...

...and continue expanding this loving energy, let it radiate from the heart until it encompasses everyone in this city where we live...embracing equally all those in pain, all those whose heart cannot yet see...breathing mercy to all beings in suffering. All those so in need of love, so in need of healing..."

Forty minutes later Darren emerges calmer than before, but still with a haunted look in his eyes. I ask him how much he remembers. "Not a cracker."

"That's fine," I say. "It's a theme I'll be returning to over the next month or two, so your unconscious will get very familiar with it." We arrange twice weekly sessions over the next month and let the book writing slide for now.

Darren's mood is low for several weeks. More tests confirm his vision is degenerating, but he has not regressed into depression, he is not paralysed. He tells me about a visit from his sister.

"Having Helen here provided a distraction, took the focus off me," he says. "I needed to pretend with her, acting upbeat as a survival strategy. I am still monitoring my sight constantly — that's very tiring. Generally things feel less severe, I'm not feeling so laboured and weighed down. A little bit lost and cranky. Not sure what to do with myself."

There is an old Sufi story, called 'The Tale of the Sands' that goes like this:[74]

There was once a stream that started up in the mountains and wound its way down and across many obstacles until finally it reached the desert. Here it sank into the sand and became a bog.

The stream is convinced its destiny is to cross the desert, yet it cannot do so. In its despair, the stream hears the voice of the desert whispering, 'just as the wind crosses the desert, so can you...' The stream objects, 'but the wind can fly...' The desert voice replies, 'allow yourself to be absorbed into the wind and the wind will carry you over... Otherwise you will become a marsh and disappear...' The stream is afraid. "Can I not remain the same stream that I am today?'

'You cannot remain so,' replies the desert. 'But the wind will take your essence up and carry you over the desert. Then, falling as rain, your essential part becomes a stream again.'

I am remembering this tale on my morning walk. Overnight rain has freshened up the air and excited the birds. It has also brought out the flies. I carry a spare t-shirt that I flick over each shoulder to swat them away. The rhythm is in time with my footfall and I begin a loose flow of thought association. I first heard this story thirty years ago. It is a simple parable, a metaphor for life, death and rebirth; about the surrender necessary to transcend pivotal moments in life. I think through various ways it might apply to Darren, or to me, or any of us. The more I analyse the story, the more it seems to lose some essential quality. To understand the story it must be heard with different ears. Not the simplistic ears of a child and not the sophisticated ears of an adult. Only right brain ears can understand the language of feeling and metaphor. At a future session, I will leave it to Darren's unconscious to make what he will of the story, to gather what is meaningful for his journey.

My path has brought me alongside paddocks of tall grasses, a legacy of the spring rains. They move as one in the breeze, a choreographed wave that travels across the fields, a shifting sea of light. Kangaroo ears appear above the forest of sun-bleached seed heads, antennae monitoring my progress. 'I come in peace,' I call to the ears, before reluctantly turning for home.

Back to our regular sessions and Darren is more upbeat, telling me about his training. "I had a nice talk with the mother of a girl who recently joined the group. She said how pleased she was with her daughter's reaction, particularly how the other kids had made her welcome. It was the whole tone of the group, the speed with which her daughter was put at ease. She has been running for several years and while I'm there she says to her Mum, 'no one's ever taught me to run before.' That still shocks me."

Darren has several of his runners in the up-coming school championships, both at state and national level. At the same time he is coaching a school football team and a ladies fitness group, a full load. There is no more news about his eye. I wonder how he can maintain the busy schedule, but he surprises me.

"It feels good to be this busy," he says. "The variety provides different challenges. I enjoy that. Definitely not about to trade. It's hard being so busy at this time of year. The lead into Christmas is hectic, but overall I welcome the challenge."

Darren continues, "I feel a sense of achievement. I spend time writing up each person's performances. I'm happy with how everyone went, several have qualified for the nationals. The footy team is going well. I'm kicking a few goals — I enjoy that." Oblivious to the pun Darren goes on, "I'm feeling pretty balanced and content. Confident sort of feeling, and competent. Nice to be able to recognise a few achievements, to see what I'm doing is working. Different to before when I would struggle to acknowledge any achievement."

Any mention of his eye is fleeting; the self-monitoring has ceased to be an obsession. Conversation invariably returns to coaching. He has two competitors in the nationals with winning chances, although he is not fazed by thoughts of triumph or glory. Darren's drive comes from the kids discovering they can do things they never thought they could do and achieving their personal best. He can be hard on them when he feels they let themselves down by not running to an agreed plan and full of praise when they run well.

Tania is running against girls a year older than herself, a tough ask at the nationals. She gets boxed in and unable to find her stride, runs a disappointing race, finishing near the back. Darren does not hold back. The plan was to stay on the outside, keeping clear of interference. Next day Tania has one more race.

This time she gets off to a quick start and opens up an early lead. Darren is riding this one, aware of his heart beat. Was he too hard on her before? The lead gets bigger until, with a lap to go, she is challenged and then overtaken by an older girl. With the rest of the field closing in on her, has Tania got anything left in the tank? She maintains her rhythm all the way over the last agonising lap, finishing second. The clock shows her beating her previous personal best by an astonishing 14 seconds. By every measure it is a huge run and she celebrates with her family. Days later in my clinic, Darren is re-living the moment, delighted for this girl he has known and trained for years. He is modest about the part he has played, but as he shares the achievement with me, I sense his unashamed pride.

With Christmas just a week away, Darren is preparing to take a holiday. He will spend a fortnight with family on the New South Wales north coast. It's been a big couple of months.

"What are you looking forward to in the holidays?" I ask.

"Some free headspace," he says. "My head has felt a bit full these last six weeks. It will be good to catch up with how I am now, how I'm handling things differently and with how I come across to other people. I've been too rushed to let it all sink in. I would like time to enjoy the contentment I've got. A bit of 'being' time."

He continues, "There are some issues to do with my eyes and the coming winter. With my sight there is a fear of the unknown. I'm uncertain if I can cope with driving at night in the winter. That will affect what training I can do. Also, I will have to make a few decisions regarding cataract surgery."

As he leaves my clinic for the last time this year he tells me, "I'd like to get back to our writing sessions next year." We shake hands, then he adds, "I'm tired, but I'm enjoying life. On balance, life is good. I'm very calm. I feel a sense of satisfaction."

Darren is more whole these days, more in touch with different parts of himself. He is lighter, less burdened; able to engage with life more broadly. He is not in denial, he still has concerns, but they no longer dominate his thinking. Darren is more resilient to life's vicissitudes. There is more balance in his thinking, more right brain influence. The changes in Darren have become grounded in the neural circuitry of his brain. His brain has learned to let go of old patterns of hyper-connectivity and is free to make new connections.

Darren is having a positive influence on those around him. The lives of his family, the lives of the young people he coaches, the lives of their parents, the lives of his small but growing circle of friends and the life of his therapist have all been touched.

A short while ago I had thought our work was over. I was preparing (a little sadly) to bring our therapy to a close. Darren's long standing condition, 'major depression and anxiety' has been addressed and is no longer present in any recognisable form. Darren has experienced excellent mental health for sufficient length of time to suggest any return to those former states is unlikely. However, I did not anticipate the sudden worsening of Darren's macular degeneration. Nor did Darren. He has managed this unexpected change in his life situation with remarkable equanimity. Sadly, the prognosis is not good, his eyesight will continue to deteriorate. While I do not doubt Darren's new found resilience, I also understand that he will need support to navigate the major transitions that lie ahead. Our work is not yet done.

Epilogue

I am sitting in Darren's kitchen, reading the final draft to him, chapter by chapter. It is the first time I have been inside Darren's place. His grandchildren's drawings decorate the walls and fridge door. There is a tin of homemade Anzac biscuits on the table. This home has a family feel.

As I read, Darren is back in his childhood. The old feelings are there again, but strong as they are, he is not consumed. This has happened a few times as we cover the early days. We talk about it and most of the time he can laugh. He will either confirm or correct me as we go through the story and fortunately, we find agreement. Writing this story has become a part of his healing.

Darren's trauma has dissolved. He no longer suffers depression. Much of his anxiety has just 'feathered away.' This is more than I dared hope for, but it is clear now that recovery did not stop there. An indefinable quality of being has developed over and above the absence of anxiety. In a very broad sense, Darren is kinder, more connected with other people and his environment. Not a saint (!) but definitely 'unfolding.' Darren referred to a time he spent 'learning to live again.' After so many years in depression he needed to catch up on life.

This second tier of recovery was possible because of Darren's willingness to continue therapy beyond a level of compromise with his depression. He took a risk to discover more about himself. Neither Darren nor I could foresee the person he is becoming. His spontaneity and humour surprise me and despite the challenges in his life he appears genuinely content most of the time. The new Darren is a product of the most mysterious drive in the universe; what the poet Kahlil Gibran calls "life's longing for itself."[75] While most obvious when we are young, this movement toward growth is present throughout life. It can sometimes be thwarted by trauma and depression, but never totally extinguished. Growth of self was re-ignited in Darren as he became free of depression, and fortified by ongoing therapy. Science cannot explain this phenomenon; not yet. It is part of the broader mystery of consciousness itself. It is intimately connected with our need for each other, for relationship, kindness and co-operation. What began as a human interest story of triumph over adversity has, in retrospect, become more of an appreciation of the innate, generative nature of the human spirit.

When observing improvements in his life, Darren often reacted with a sense of awe, exclaiming, "...but how it happened I don't know." Darren was mystified by what was happening to him, because it was the outcome of his *unconscious* intelligence. In the past Darren had put great effort into doing his assigned homework and following the logical strategies, convinced his failure to get better was down to his lack of application. He had to try harder. Now, in the absence of strategies and having done nothing (in his view) other than turn up for meditation and storytelling each week, he experiences this remarkable improvement. In a world of Newtonian physics his recovery was pure magic.

Today, science has a different view. Affective neuroscience has proven the primacy of unconscious feelings over cognitive process. Thanks to modern science we can witness the brain working to dissolve painful feelings during REM sleep. If for any reason, this 'overnight therapy' is not effectively carried out, the undissolved emotions become toxic and affect the different physical systems of the body, forming the basis of anxiety and in severe cases, depression. Seen in this way, neuroscience offers an explanation for depression and, by extension, an account of how Darren's depression was feathered away by a therapy that mimics the effect of REM sleep.

When it comes to unfolding we are still in the age of wonder. Science is light years away from explaining the second tier of Darren's recovery. The unconscious intelligence that directs our self-healing, self-organising, self-generating and endlessly creative mind remains a mystery to be celebrated. Darren doesn't know how it happened because he didn't do it. Not in a deliberate, egoic sense. I did not do it either, although I was there, of course; my presence was part of the process. None of us do this on our own. Unconscious intelligence is at play throughout our lives, vital in our ability to heal and to survive.

In writing this story I have come to a greater appreciation of my own unconscious at work. Those sudden insights and new connections that came, seemingly unbidden, to my mind. Like the time I was listening to Professor Russell Meares describe dissociation as a pathology, caused by a disorganisation of the cerebral function due to overwhelming trauma. In that moment I suddenly understood that depression was a partial collapse of the nervous system, brought about by overwhelming anxiety. A few days later, I was re-visiting Meares' book, *Intimacy and Alienation*, and I was surprised to find that years earlier I had read and highlighted the section on dissociation and trauma, I had even made notes in the margin.[76] It seems that back then my unconscious mind was not ready to make the intuitive leap between dissociation, trauma and depression! That moment of intuition nudged me toward uncommon research such as the traumatic memory system and functional hyper-connectivity; in turn this led me to creative understandings like 'the brain that can't let go.'

Whether mental, physical or emotional, all healing is unconscious, the wonders of modern medicine notwithstanding. Healing is as natural as breathing. We need look no further than the placebo effect as proof, occurring daily whenever we believe a pill will cure our ills. The belief itself is a sufficient stimulus for the self-healing resources to kick into action and do their job, regardless of the chemical make-up of the pill. It is our relationship with the person prescribing the pill that frames our mindset and determines our belief in the remedy. Every new medication is tested against a placebo to measure its efficacy. My own experience of placebo began when I was very young.

Epilogue

As a boy I regularly wet the bed. It was embarrassing and prevented me from going on sleepovers and camps with my friends for many years. I tried all sorts of gadgets that would wake me up in time, but they never did. Eventually my mother arranged for me to see a specialist in London.

The room is large and smells funny. He glances down from his desk in my direction and I look at the floor, pretending not to see him. At first I wonder if he is coming over to sit on the bench next to me, but no, he pulls a chair to the side of the podium and sits down. I shuffle into the corner with a tinge of disappointment. The windows behind his desk reveal the gloomy city light. Sitting opposite in a semi-circle is a group of earnest young men, eagerly clutching notebooks and pens. A few minutes ago they watched me enter without warmth or acknowledgement. I am on my own, the focus of attention. The great man speaks in a bass voice:

"Ah… Michael, welcome. These other people are my students. They are here to observe; you should ignore them." As if. "Tell me about the bed wetting. How often does it happen?" He asks a number of questions most of which I can't answer, my mouth is so dry. I try not to look at the students and hope I don't wet my pants. The great man runs out of questions and sits thoughtfully. After an age he bursts into action, throwing open the top draw of his desk with a flourish, producing a small glass bottle.

"I want you to take one of these pills every night before you go to bed. Keep taking them until they run out. Don't forget, one every night. You won't have a problem after that." I detect the first trace of warmth in his voice. From nowhere a woman appears to usher me out of the room with my little bottle of magic pills. "Why didn't Dr Jackson (my GP) give me these in the first place?" I ask Mum on the way home. She shrugs.

I never knew what she thought, but she maintained the charade and reminded me every night to take my medicine. I stopped wetting the bed from that moment. It was many years later that I finally twigged there were no medicines that stopped you wetting the bed. Fortunately the great man and his little bottle of pills had done their job by then. He understood the mind better than most and I must have been impressed by his assurance that I could stay dry at night. Were his actions ethical? I am glad I don't have to answer that; suffice to say he did no harm, he didn't change me and yet the desired outcome was achieved. What do placebos have in common with P.S.H.? Both point to the self-healing nature of our being, confirming all healing is unconscious. Interestingly, both indicate the importance of relationship in enabling healing to flourish.

The time spent working with Darren and writing this book has taught me to recognise my limitations; to let go of my delusions and my impatience. No therapist can change another person; hence Darren's intuitive plea, 'don't ask me to change.' No therapist can heal another person. At its best, therapy employs skilful means to *facilitate* the unfolding and the autonomic, regenerative functions within the client. There were months when nothing seemed to change and at times I did become impatient with the tools I was using, and wondered whether I needed something 'stronger.' Thankfully it never came to that; as Darren pointed out, it wasn't a crow bar he needed, ultimately the rock in his chest was feathered away. I learned over the course of our therapy that the most powerful tool in the clinic room was the sense of trust, the belief we had in each other. Magic happened as we began to listen to the unspoken intimations coming from our collective unconscious.

In Freud's day, a therapist would tell us about ourselves, interpret our dreams for us and decipher our hidden motivations through practices such as word association. For Freud, the therapist was an intermediary who could explore our unconscious thoughts on our behalf and tell us what was needed in order for us to be healed. This was massively empowering for the therapist; less so for the client. A basic principle of Freudian psychoanalysis was to make the unconscious conscious, but it was the therapist doing the making *on behalf of the client*. This type of intervention is problematic. Success is dependent not only upon the accuracy of the therapist's interpretation, but also on how well the patient receives the therapist's view of them! Freud's concept of the unconscious as a repository of painful memories that affect our daily thinking and behaviour was revolutionary for his time. However, it was a decidedly partial conclusion. He gave little credit to the regenerative, creative and healing capacity that is the true wonder of consciousness. More than 80 years after Freud's death, this diminished view of our unconscious mind remains dominant; a container full of all the yucky stuff we would rather not know about. Unfortunately, it is a view that adds to the stigma associated with mental illness. The unconscious mind has been seriously misrepresented.

This book brings a new perspective; the unconscious mind that started off as the villain of the piece now ends up as the hero. Our unconscious intelligence, woven inextricably within the right hemisphere of the brain, is the source of our redemptive power for healing. It was not magical thinking that transformed Darren's life. Action was needed. The nature of this action was cooperative, right brain to right brain communication. This was difficult in the beginning because there was not much happening in Darren to communicate with. Such is the nature of depression. It was through voice guided meditation, relaxation and cooperative communion that things began to develop. Storytelling provided the means of communicating with Darren's unconscious, which in turn led to the release of shackles that he had locked in place and to which only he held the key.

It is impossible to measure the depth of pain inflicted on humanity by anxiety and depression. Measurements are numbers and numbers don't feel pain. According to Beyond Blue, one in seven Australians currently experience anxiety.[77] That is a huge number of people — about 2.7 million. The real figure could be far more than that. Without a satisfactory definition of anxiety how do we know what we are measuring? Many people are averse to seeking help, while others are part of the 'invisible face' cohort who, like Darren, do not think they are anxious. If you include these people in the data, we are possibly looking at double that number — about 5.4 million and growing fast. What stands in the way of tackling this growing pandemic? You've guessed it; our left brain dominated culture, with its disrespect for our unconscious emotional nature. Out of that culture of ignorance come many health and medical leaders, stubbornly blind to the new and inconvenient truth of affective neuroscience. OK, that maybe harsh. In truth, we are all captive to the collective mindset within which we grow and learn. When you have a lifetime understanding the world from a left brain perspective — when that is your lived experience — you simply have no choice; right brain principles and unconscious communication might just as well have come from another planet.

Today, our rising individual levels of anxiety are reflected in our governments, in social media and institutions. Insecure, we seek in vain for reassurance and certainty. Over a decade ago, Iain McGilchrist predicted how society would change for the worse as we move inexorably toward left brain dominance:

> "...increasingly the living would be modelled on the mechanical; quantity would be the only criteria and the Right's appreciation of quality would be lost...along with one's integrity as a unique individual subject...The left hemisphere prefers the impersonal...which would come to replace the personal. There would be focus on the material things at the expense of the living...exploitation rather than co-operation...social cohesion neglected, disrupted..."[78]

When we operate in a largely left brain dominated world of purely 'logical' thinking, there is little time for contemplation; no place for right brain cohesion and no appreciation of unconscious thought. Our left brain operates to manipulate the environment, to provide the certainty and control for us to survive and prosper. The whisperings of unconscious thinking are mocked by left brain triumphalism and wither in the face of the onslaught. The history of civilisation since the industrial revolution shows how economically successful left brain domination has been. Only now are we beginning to realise the cost we are all paying in terms of social fragmentation, loneliness, mental ill-health and environmental degradation.

In contrast, the currency of right brain consciousness is *potential*; the boundless potential for connection, cohesion, belonging, creativity and regeneration, none of which are measurable, because to measure would place limits and there are no limits. For the same reason, none of these qualities have a predictable certainty.

We need balance. We need both halves of our brain fully operational for mental health to flourish and for our lives to prosper, so we can remain wholly connected with nature's boundless creativity. Both individually and collectively, we need right brain focus to help bring healing to ourselves and the world. This need has never been more urgent.

A great peacemaker awaits us in the form of contemplative practice. It has been interesting to witness the rise in popularity of mindfulness, chiefly because of its calming, right brain dominant focus. Elsewhere some alternative antidotes are emerging. Animals figure prominently here, particularly horses and dogs. War veterans with PTSD are finding healing and peace as they form a bond with their equine companion. Similarly, others are invited to adopt a canine friend to care for. As far as I am aware, these animals do not engage in rational thought. It is a different kind of relationship that opens us up to right brain process, providing a bridge of love to reconnect us with our implicit, unconscious nature.

Like many others, I find therapy in the garden, in the feel of damp earth, the delight of new life emerging, the first blossoms of spring, in welcoming birds when they visit, some briefly, others staying to nest in the thickets. It is through the processes of the right hemisphere that our hearts learn to sing again. There was a slogan back in the 80s, 'inner peace, world peace.' This is a helpful focus for me during difficult times. When despairing at the state of the world, I still find meditating or walking in nature restores my equilibrium. Most of the time. Another antidote to our collective imbalance is to work for a cause bigger than ourselves. Volunteering appears to bring many benefits for the human heart, more so than if we were being paid for the same work.

Of all the different ways to access right brain states, meditation in its various forms is considered the most helpful for the most number of people. In this regard, music and art sometimes become forms of meditation. Unconscious intelligence is not competitive and in that sense it is not egoic; it experiences the natural world as essentially cooperative, inter connected and inter dependent. It is fundamentally involved in healing, regenerating and creative, original thought. Awareness and trust are two vital elements needed to nurture this aspect of our mind. A regular contemplative practice will provide the opportunity for both.

However many people are too anxious to meditate, finding the experience of isolation confronting; there is a fear of letting down their guard and a need to refocus on the many hurts and threats in their life. There is talk these days about the downside of mindfulness, with reports that some people are suffering panic attacks as a result of the practice. I developed voice-guided meditation for precisely this reason, so people feel they are connected with me and can trust the process. The effect of the human voice can be enormously helpful when we need to let go. The stories I tell form an alternative focus for the restless mind, leading to a state of deep rest and minimal thinking. This state is the very opposite to panic or anxiety. It is not dependent on technique or left brain narrow focus, it is the realm of the right brain, effortless and restorative.

If you find meditation or mindfulness difficult, try looking for a teacher who uses voice and story to guide you into meditation; someone you feel you can trust. Alternatively, I have a number of voice-guided meditation recordings that are available on iTunes and my website. There are some who claim this is not *real* meditation. My response is simple. This works. People can find peace of mind — even someone suffering major depression and anxiety for as long as Darren had. Ideally, I recommend P.S.H. therapy in conjunction with a meditation practice you find calming.

Darren's story is an astounding one; one that I hope will arouse some curiosity in the mental health world. Darren continues to enjoy a good quality of life. At a time where many people are feeling increased anxiety, he continues to meet the ongoing challenges in his life with good humour and it has been a long time since he felt depressed. He offers me another Anzac biscuit and looks me in the eye. I know what he is going to say. "Have we got a publisher yet?"

None of the material I present in this story is new. In fact, the science has been in the public domain for a number of years. Yet, to the best of my knowledge, others have not made the same creative connections that I have made with the available information. My unique understanding is due in no small part to witnessing Darren's journey out of anxiety and depression — the deeply personal and lived insights that can't be gleaned from scientific research or texts. It is also a result of my vocation — as a therapist whose life's work is focussed on the subconscious, I am adept at searching for light in dark places. I offer this book as a contribution to our collective understanding of depression and anxiety. The conclusions I draw are original. They are prescient in today's world.

At times I am amazed at where I find myself today. I said at the start of the story that I never set out to be a therapist and yet here I am. Working with clients nourishes me; always stimulating, often challenging and immensely rewarding. Hopefully the journey has a way to go yet. I have deep gratitude for whoever directed me here and the greatest respect for the underlying intelligence that still nudges me on to new experiences, renewing me every day.

Endnotes

Chapter 1: Michael and Darren
1. Barnett, E. (1979). *Unlock your mind and be free! A practical approach to hypnotherapy*. Dominie: Toronto
2. Levine, S. (1991). *Guided Meditations, Explorations and Healings*. Gateway Books. p.32
3. Rogers, C. R. (1961). *On Becoming a Person: A Therapist's View of Psychotherapy*. Boston: Houghton Mifflin Company

Chapter 2: No Ordinary Sadness
4. Fry, Stephen (2015). What not to say to a depressed person. https://archive.attn.com/stories/3548/stephen-fry-depression. Accessed 10/11/2019.
5. Conington, J. (1863). *The Satires, Epistles, and Art of Poetry of Horace*. London: George Bell & Sons, p.90.

Chapter 3: A Complicating Factor
6. Levine, S. (1991). *Guided Meditations, Explorations and Healings*. Gateway Books. p.260
7. Meares, R. (2013). Keynote Speech at the 2013 Australia and New Zealand Association of Psychotherapy Annual Conference. Sydney
8. Nestler, E. (2016). Depression is driven by networks of genes that span brain circuits. Science Daily. <https://www.sciencedaily.com/releases/2016/05/160512130508.htm> Accessed 13/05/2016
9. Burnside, N. (2020). ANU Researchers Discover Swelling of part of the Brain in People with both Depression and Anxiety. ABC News <Australian National University researchers discover swelling of part of the brain in people with both depression and anxiety — ABC News> Accessed 7/08/2020

Chapter 4: Don't Mention the Feelings
10. Wilber, K. (2000). *Integral Psychology*. Shambala Boston & London
11. Planck M. (1949). *Scientific Autobiography*. Philosophical Library. p.33
12. Panksepp, J. as quoted in Schore A. (2012). *The Science of the Art of Psychotherapy*. Norton. p.4
13. Schore A. (2012). *The Science of the Art of Psychotherapy*. Norton. p.3
14. Ibid. p.3
15. Verny, T. (2002). *Pre-Parenting... Nurturing your Child from Conception*. Simon & Schuster New York. p.112
16. Australia and New Zealand Association of Psychotherapy (ANZAP). The Conversational Method. < https://www.anzap.com.au/index.php/about-anzap/anzap/about-the-conversational-model> Accessed 1/5/2014

17   Schore A. (2012). *The Science of the Art of Psychotherapy*. Norton. p.5
18   Xiang Cai, et al. (2013). *Depression stems from miscommunication between brain cells*. University of Maryland Medical Centre.
19   Calmbirth. < https://calmbirth.com.au/> Accessed 11/7/2016
20   Raisanen, S. et al. (2013) Risk factors for and perinatal outcomes of major depression during pregnancy: a population-based analysis during 2002-2010 in Finland. BMJ Open 2014;4:11 e004883.

Chapter 5: The Brain That Can't Let Go

21   Leuchter, A. (2012) Hyperactivity in brain may explain multiple symptoms of depression. ScienceDaily. <www.sciencedaily.com/releases/2012/02/120227162656.htm> Accessed 24/3/2016
22   Langenecker, S. et al. Emotion-processing networks disrupted in sufferers of depression. University of Illinois at Chicago. ScienceDaily, 20 January 2016. www.sciencedaily.com/releases/2016/01/160120143007.htm Accessed 23/3/2016
23   Levine, S. (1991). *Guided Meditations, Explorations and Healings*. Gateway Books. p.259
24   Van der Helm, E. and Walker, M. (December 2011) REM Sleep Depotentiates Amygdala Activity to Previous Emotional Experiences, Current Biology, Volume 21, Issue 23.

Chapter 6: The Tigers Keep Coming Back

25   Kabat-Zinn, J. (1994). *Wherever You Go There You Are*. Hyperion
26   Damasio, A. (1999). *The Feeling of What Happens*. Mariner Books p.56
27   Shakespeare, W. Macbeth — the Witches Song. https://www.poetryfoundation.org/poems/43189/song-of-the-witches-double-double-toil-and-trouble Accessed 10/11/2019
28   Meares, R. (2000). *Intimacy and Alienation*. Bruner-Routledge. p.80
29   LeDoux, J. (1996). *The Emotional Brain*. Simon and Schuster. p.203

Chapter 7: My Own Person

30   LeDoux, J. (1996). *The Emotional Brain*. Simon and Schuster. pp.242-300
31   Damasio, A. (1999). *The Feeling of What Happens*. Mariner Books p.56
32   LeDoux, J. (1996). *The Emotional Brain*. Simon and Schuster. p.94

Chapter 8: The Four Faces of Anxiety

33   LeDoux, J. (1996). *The Emotional Brain*. Simon and Schuster. p.203
34   Ibid. p.242
35   Boomtown Rats (1979) *I Don't Like Mondays*. https://www.youtube.com/watch?v=xSFIPcwqGvw Accessed 14/08/2019
36   Justice McLennan, P. Speaking at the Australian and New Zealand Association of Psychotherapists (ANZAP) Annual Conference September 2017.

Chapter 9: No Moorings

37   Shakespeare W. Macbeth. https://www.enotes.com/homework-help/what-does-macbeth-mean-when-he-says-macbeth-does-465943 Accessed 10/01/2019
38   Van der Helm, E. and Walker, M. (September 2009) A convergent view of sleep-dependent emotional brain processing. Volume 135(5) pp.731-748.

Chapter 10: Voices in the Head

39 Erickson, M. (1982) *My Voice Will Go With You — The Teaching Tales Of Milton H Erickson*. W. W. Norton
40 Erickson, M. https://www.goodreads.com/author/quotes/79897.Milton_H_Erickson Accessed 10/01/2019
41 Ashcroft-Nowicki, D. (1999). *The Initiates Book of Pathworkings*. Samuel Weiser. p 201
42 Levine, S. (1991). *Guided Meditations, Explorations and Healings*. Gateway Books. p.259.
43 Philostratus, Life of Apollonius of Tyana. https://www.livius.org/sources/content/philostratus-life-of-apollonius/philostratus-life-of-apollonius-5.11-15/#5.14 Accessed 24/07/2018
44 Aesop. (1867). *The Fox Without a Tail*. Aesop's Fables (Lit2Go Edition). https://etc.usf.edu/lit2go/35/aesops-fables/608/the-fox-without-a-tail/ Accessed 30/03/2019
45 Wilde, O., and Robinson, C. (1920). *The happy prince: And other tales*. New York: Brentano's.
46 Potter, B. (2002). *The Tale of Peter Rabbit*. London: Frederick Warne.
47 Adler, C. (1987). Relaxation induced Panic (RIP). Integrative Psychiatry 5 pp. 94-100 as quoted in Burkeman. O, (2012). The Antidote. Text Publishing: Melbourne. p.15
48 Walter Bellin Partnership. (1981) Being Up Front: Drama course. Sydney
49 Trevarthen, C. Professor. Keynote speaker at ANZAP (Australia and New Zealand Association of Psychotherapists) annual conferences, Sydney 2014 and 2011.
50 Trevarthen, C. and Malloch, S. (Eds) (2009) *Communicative Musicality*. Oxford University Press.
51 Crapo, T. (2014) Carol Purington's dreaming room. https://www.recorder.com/Archives/2013/12/Book-122813-GR-Crapo-purington Accessed 12/09/2017

Chapter 11: Feathered Away

52 BBC (1999) Michael Parkinson interviews Paul McCartney https://www.youtube.com/watch?v=SzDNbjBm0bM Accessed 1/03/2019
53 McGreevey, S. (2011) Eight Weeks to a Better Brain. Harvard Gazette http://news.harvard.edu/gazette/story/2011/01/eight-weeks-to-a-better-brain Accessed 22/03/2013
54 Khoury, B., Lecomte, T., Fortin, G., Masse, M., Therien, P., Bouchard, V., Chapleau, M. A., Paquin, K., & Hofmann, S. G. (2013). Mindfulness-based therapy: A comprehensive meta-analysis. Clinical Psychology Review, 33, 763–771.
55 Segal, Z. V., Williams, J. M. G. & Teasdale, J. T. (2012). *Mindfulness-Based Cognitive Therapy for Depression*. (2nd ed.). New York: The Guilford Press.
56 Kabat-Zinn, J. (2013). *Full Catastrophe Living: Using the Wisdom of Your Body and Mind to Face Stress, Pain, and Illness*. Westminster, MD: Bantam.
57 Arkowitz, H. and Lilienfeld, S. (2014, September/October). Is Mindfulness Good Medicine? Scientific American, 5(25), pp. 74–75. www.scientificamerican.com/article/is-mindfulness-good-medicine. Accessed 2/11/2016
58 Freud. S. (1920-22) Two encyclopaedia articles (A) Psychoanalysis. Cited in Meares, R. (2005) *The Metaphor of Play* (3rd Edition). Routledge. p.123
59 McGilchrist, I. (2010). *The Master and his Emissary*. Yale University Press.
60 Meares, R. (2012). *A Dissociation Model of Borderline Personality Disorder*. Norton. p.289

Chapter 12: Don't Ask Me to Change

61 Jung C.G. (1977). Vol. 18, p.175, as cited in Meares, R. (2016). *The Poet's Voice and the Making of Mind.* Routledge. p 171.
62 Letter from Pauli, W. to Jung, C.G. (1949) as cited in Meares, R. (2016). *The Poet's Voice and the Making of Mind.* Routledge. p.178.
63 Meares, R. (2016). *The Poet's Voice and the Making of Mind.* Routledge. p.182.
64 Rumi, https://www.azquotes.com/quote/464757 Accessed 08/04/2020

Chapter 13: The Halfway House

65 Poincaré, H. (1913). *The Foundations of Science.* (Translated by G.B. Halsted.) New York: Science Press. pp. 383 — 394.
66 Snyder, A. et al. (2009). The Incubation Effect: Hatching a Solution? Creativity Research Journal, 21(1), pp.6-14.
67 Knox, J. (2011). *Self-Agency in Psychotherapy.* WW Norton. p.37.
68 Karmiloff-Smith, A. (1992). *Beyond Modularity.* MIT Press.
69 Ibid. p 20.
70 Ibid. p 18.

Chapter 14: The Emerging Self

71 Blagrove, M. et al. New Scientist. No:3187: 21 July 2018
72 Ibid. p.4.
73 Levine, S. (1991). *Guided Meditations, Explorations and Healings.* Gateway Books. p.290.
74 Shah, I. (1993). *Tales of the Dervishes.* Penguin.

Epilogue

75 Gibran, K. (1979). *The Prophet.* Heinemann: London
76 Meares, R. (2000). *Intimacy and Alienation.* Bruner-Routledge. p.44
77 Beyond Blue < Anxiety, depression and suicide prevention support — Beyond Blue> Accessed 13/05/2020
78 McGilchrist, I. (2010). *The Master and his Emissary.* Yale University Press. pp.429 — 431

www.ingramcontent.com/pod-product-compliance
Lightning Source LLC
Chambersburg PA
CBHW022046290426
44109CB00014B/1007